SPIRITUALITY AND PRAYER: JEWISH AND CHRISTIAN UNDERSTANDINGS

Edited by

Leon Klenicki
and
Gabe Huck

A Stimulus Book

Paulist Press ■ New York ■ Ramsey

Library of Congress
Catalog Card Number: 82-62966

ISBN: 0-8091-2538-2

Published by Paulist Press
545 Island Road, Ramsey, N.J. 07446

Printed and bound in the
United States of America

SPIRITUALITY AND PRAYER: JEWISH AND CHRISTIAN UNDERSTANDINGS

Studies in Judaism and Christianity

Exploration of Issues in the Contemporary Dialogue Between Christians and Jews

Contents

1.
Exile and Return: Moments in the Jewish Pilgrimage to God

Leon Klenicki

Jewish spirituality is a meeting, an encounter entailing two dimensions. One is the covenantal relationship God-Israel, the other its implementation in a daily actualization of the experience of God, His Call and Presence, in individual and community existence.

There is no precise theological expression for spirituality in Hebrew, though two terms should be considered: *Halakha* and *Emuna. Halakha,* wrongly translated as law, *nomos,* by the biblical and Latin translators, is a way of being and doing, a means of implementing the covenantal relationship. *Emuna,* faith, is the experience of reliving the covenantal relationship, and an attitude of the spirit, of hope and realization. *Emuna* and *Halakha* convey the whole range of Jewish spirituality.

Jewish spirituality is expressed, for instance, in the star of David, a symbol employed by Franz Rosenzweig, the twentieth century German Jewish religious thinker, in his book *The Star of Redemption.*[1] The two triangles of the star express central ideas of Jewish commitment. The first triangle points to the concepts of God, the Promise of making Israel a people with a vocation of service to the world, and the Promised Land. The second triangle indicates steps in the realization of Jewish spirituality: Revelation, the gift of Creation, and the Kingdom of God, i.e., the word of God implemented in history.

The Spirituality of Creation

The experience of God is an encounter—God-person, God-community—conveying a transformation of self, a conversion of being. The experience can be mystical or para-normal, though generally of a regenerative nature. God is perceived, received as a Presence and a Commanding Voice, a Wholesome Holiness felt as a reality outside the self.

Creation is such an experience. The account of creation in the Book of Genesis is neither a scientific response, nor a physical explanation of the world, as are, e.g., the ideological explorations of Greek philosophy. The biblical author goes beyond any scientific theory, to relate an idea linked to God's plan and vision. Creation, according to later rabbinic concepts, is God's blueprint, preceding the world itself, intended to circumscribe the dominion of person and community. It is not a capricious gift of God, but His actualization of a meaningful purpose, a call to human commitment, a way to be followed by the individual person himself.

Creation implies a human obligation, a commitment to God's present of life, to keep, to honor, and thereby ever expanding its possibilities and dimensions. This commitment is ever-present in prayer. The morning service, after the blessing of God, declares the formation of light and darkness and all things proclaiming the renewal of the daily work of creation. Creation entails a unique experience of God, a Presence that commands and the word becomes reality. Creation establishes conditions, e.g., the forbidden fruit mentioned in Genesis 2, and decides the future of the transgressors, Adam and Eve, who are paradigmatic for all mankind. God is sensed as Creator, establishing a friendship, not yet a covenant, with Noah and his family, to save a remnant of humanity, despite human evil. God is experienced as a *numinous,* a *Mysterium Tremendum.* Rudolf Otto describes this element of the experience of God, at present in crisis among contemporary Jews, informing the theistic concept of God:

> The feeling of it may at times come sweeping like a gentle tide, pervading the mind with a tranquil mood of deepest worship. It may pass over into a more set and lasting attitude of the soul, continuing, as it were, thrillingly vibrant and resonant, until at last it dies away and the soul resumes its "profane", non-religious mood of everyday experience. It may burst in sudden eruption up from the depths of the soul with spasms and convulsions, or lead to the strangest excitements, to intoxicated frenzy, to transport, and to ecstasy. It has its wild and demonic forms and can sink to an almost grisly horror and shuddering. It has its

> crude, barbaric antecedents and early manifestations, and again it may be developed into something beautiful and pure and glorious. It may become the hushed, trembling, and speechless humility of the creature in the presence of—whom or what? In the presence of that which is a *mystery* inexpressible and above all creatures.[2]

The numinous experience of God, a process of inner growth, and awareness permeates all biblical accounts, and was expounded in rabbinic commentary responding to historical realities.

The Spirituality of a Call

The basic example of the total experience of God is Abram's call, as narrated in Genesis 12. The first verses narrate the inner transformation of the person in contact with God, undergoing an encounter of revelation. The call involves a change and a promise. Abram's life is transformed by accepting God's command, leaving his country and family, two basic elements of the human condition.

The Promise carries along two angles: the obligation to become a *goi gadol,* a community with a vocation and a destiny; and a Promised Land, the national center of worship and identification. The experience of God's overwhelming presence is followed, first, by a change of name, Abram to Abraham, Sarai to Sarah, and, second, by the establishment of sacrifices. The change of name denotes the centrality of the experience of God. Names were since early days safe-conducts in the Middle East identifying the person, his family connections, his history. A change of name means a new beginning, even a new life. Accepting God is this new beginning.

Abram in his inner transformation faces a crisis. It is a crucial, vital situation, a turning point. His life is changed materially and spiritually; a new road lies ahead of him and his family. God's word is the crisis of a call, an invitation to meaningful existence, a change in the rhythm of time, an either/or election. With Abraham's call begins a sequence of individual and national crises in Judaism that deeply affect the course of its spirituality. Those times of crisis will be of varying proportion and relate to historical events. A crisis is not a time of decadence, though it may occur in such a period. It is a process of conversion, a deepening of the faith meaning, and a response in religious commitment. Crisis is a crossroad of faith.

Abram went into exile from the idol worship of his family's pantheon. God's call turned him toward a relationship with the Source of all meaning, changing his life and purpose. Abraham began the living experience of exile and return that informs Jewish life and spirituality throughout history.

The story of Abraham is not presented as an historical reality in the Bible but as a reflection, a prototype to follow in personal religious development. Abraham is singled out, spoken to and sent out. He must go away, on his own, searching, doubting, and asking. He, like any religious person touched by God's presence, is isolated, alone but not alienated, witnessing God in history, testifying to the covenantal relationship.

Abraham becomes a model community for the nations. He is not considered a righteous man, but he and his people are destined to become righteous in time and history. Abraham is commanded "to walk before Me," in contrast to Noah who "walked with God." God's command implies the task of proclaiming His Name and to live within God's covenantal alliance. Noah appears as representative of a nationless humanity. Abraham has the vocation to establish God's chosen people; he and all of Israel witness God to humanity until the messianic time of gathering all peoples to the Mountain of the Lord (Is 2:1–5). Abraham's spirtuality connotes in every generation the experience of God, in a call, in a crisis of vocation; however it presents itself, it means a renewal of inner life, an abandonment of the comfort of ideological frames, the protective shield of common places; it also connotes the reality of a Promised Land. Abraham projects a sense of loneliness by following the call of God, but also the obligation to witness and to belong to the community of faith. Abraham basically represents the essence of Jewish spirituality.

CRISIS AND HISTORY: SPIRITUALITIES OF RETURN

The primordial experience of exile is the Egyptian slavery. The Book of Exodus relates the events leading to Pharaoh's dictatorship and Jewish slavery. The account stands as paradigmatic symbol for all times of exile, as well as for a call to Jewish responsibility in reshaping religious existence.

The Exodus event involves two stages that are repeated in successive historical episodes: the political aspect, the outer dimension, and a consequent spiritual renewal. Moses, appointed by God for the mission of liberation, carries the community from a land of slavery to the desert, toward a cleansing of the heart, and toward the Land. Political liberation achieves its apex at the Mount Sinai gathering, the revelational encounter with God, the establishment of a sacred alliance. Sinai stands for the covenantal relationship God-Israel, a totality of outer and inner freedom.

The spirituality of Exodus, exile and return, implies reaching an historical wholeness rooted in the memory of slavery, past and present, and in inner liberation. It is God's commanding voice at Sinai: a commitment to a moral code shaping existence in its individual and communal reality. The fullness of redemption is relived every year in the Passover celebration. The *Haggadah,*[3] the liturgy for the occasion, stresses various aspects of redemption: the liberation, the obligation to transmit this heritage from one generation to another (the Four Questions); the obligation to share food and shelter with the stranger and the poor; *Ha Lahma,* the bread of affliction; the narration of slavery; the recital of Hallel Psalms, 115–118; the partaking of the cup of Elijah with its messianic overtones; and finally the hope of return to Jerusalem, *Leshana haba birushalaim,* next year in Jerusalem, that has become a reality in the twentieth century.

Another crisis experience of exile and return is the Babylonian exile. Nebuchadnezzar, king of Babylon, took Jerusalem in 586 BCE and sent nearly all its population to exile in his country. Biblical sources portrayed God's design as a punishment for the city's transgressions (Jer 34:2f). Lamentations 1:1–3 conveys dramatically the despair of the people, abandoned, without the consolation of the beloved city, and the salvific sacrificial system. Israel has become, as defined in Psalm 137:1–6, a nation in exile, alienated, dreaming of a city, Jerusalem, their very center of being and essence. All these feelings are relived at the yearly commemoration of *Tishah b'Av,* the ninth of the month of Av, that recalls in ritual and spirituality the destruction of the Temple and the days of destruction, throughout the centuries, up to the diabolic days of the Holocaust. The spirituality of that day becomes a symbol for all days, combining history and memory, destruction and the eternal hope in God's Promise.[4]

The Jewish people in Babylonia was faced with the dilemma of continuing the covenantal relationship in prayer and meditation, or to disappear among the society at large. The community had to pass through a time of soul reckoning, and consideration of past mistakes and transgressions; they had to purify themselves, to advance toward interior resurrection and a revival of bones, as in the image of Ezekiel 37. The people of Israel had to recognize the human alienation of history, but God's eternal Presence and the reality of the covenantal relationship limit-situation sustained them. A new spirituality, a way of manifesting God, was to be born in the midst of the deportation. It was a return to the source: re-encountering God in a renewal of hope.[5] Jeremiah testified to the recognition of that situation and the need to witness God:

> Thus said the Lord of Hosts, the God of Israel, to the whole community which I exiled from Jerusalem to Babylon: Build houses and live in them, plant gardens and eat their fruit. Take wives and beget sons and daughters; and take wives for your sons, and give your daughters to husbands, that they may bear sons and daughters. Multiply there, do not decrease, and seek the welfare of the city to which I have exiled you and pray to the Lord in its behalf; for in its prosperity you shall prosper (29:47).

Both Ezekiel and Jeremiah, who had personally experienced exile, express the messianic hope of a return. Both compose a theme of spiritual transformation and renewal, touching upon two dimensions: the establishment of a new covenant, and growth in understanding God (Jer 31:31–40) and the return to the Promised Land (Ez 11:17–20).

The post-exilic covenant renews the Sinaitic situation, enriching it with the experience of Babylon and a personal spirituality of "dry bones" that serves to overcome despair and historical reality. The new covenant finds fulfillment in Ezra and Nehemiah's expounding of the biblical text and the community's recovery of its own soil and sacred city, Jerusalem. The exilic covenant is a relationship of friendship based on new beginnings: God forgiving past transgressions (Jer 31:34) though asking for prior repentance (36:3) and turning away from past mistakes (24:7; also 1 Kgs 8:37–39). The new covenant is written on the heart of the people instead of stones (Ex 20), entailing an obligation to understand its meaning. While Deuteronomy uses technical juridical words, ordinances and statutes, to describe the covenantal content, the redactor of Jeremiah uses words of pivotal significance in the prophet's message: the covenant is a gift of the Spirit that requires elaboration by Israel. A spirituality of hope is born, in search for the meaning of God, and an affirmative response to exile and alienation follow from it. By accepting historical reality, Israel could understand God's predicate: "They shall be my people and I will be their God" (Jer 31:33; 32:38).

King Cyrus' decree (Ezra 6:3–5) allowed the prisoners in Babylon to return to Jerusalem. It is a time of restoration, a search for new meanings.

The return implies the process of rebuilding the city of Jerusalem and its Temple; it also entails the interior reshaping of the covenantal relationship. This process of re-forming the interior and exterior aspects of Judaism started a spirituality that would last for several centuries, until the destruction of the Temple by the Romans in the year 70 CE.

Ezra and Nehemiah understood, as did the other prophets, that the construction of the Temple dedicated to God should also be an inner process. Sinai must continue under changed circumstances and historical realities. The new covenant, foretold by Jeremiah, requires a new understanding of God's word, call and promises. At a holy convocation (Neh 8) the text is read and expounded, making the people aware of its basic message. The understanding of the text is facilitated by "bringing nearer the somewhat remote in it, paraphrasing an older statement, substantially repeating the gist of the document thus explained."[6] The readings and comments by Ezra reshape the biblical text, actualizing its message in a tense situation, "between continuation and rebellion, tradition and convocation." It is, as Simon Rawidowicz pointed out, "a revolution from within, planned and executed by insiders with a purpose of reshaping their home."[7]

Nehemiah 8 exemplifies the expounding of a biblical text as a living experience of the word of God. *Torah* becomes the vital guideline for the post-exilic community upon its return to the Promised Land. *Torah,* teaching, projects ways of moral and ethical conduct, daily spirituality, the sanctification of personal and national existence, the *imitatio Dei.* The spirituality of the restoration is not legalistic but a way, a means to manifest and implement the experience of God, according to the Sinai revelation and subsequent historical experience. It is *Halakha* (from the verb *halakh,* to go). As already mentioned, the noun can be translated as "a way of being, a way of going." It is not law, as mistranslated by the Alexandria school and taken over by the Church Fathers, in confrontation with the synagogue. *Halakha* is not legalism, but a way, a spirituality rooted in Sinai. It developed over five centuries of search, transmitted from one generation to another, was enlarged upon by teachers, the men of the synagogue, and finally canonized in the year 200 CE. The destruction of the Temple in the year 70 gave the final thrust to the *halakhic* process that would continue as normative rule through modern times, and is suffering a crisis in the twentieth century, the period before and after the exile of the Holocaust.

EXTERIOR EXILE AND INTERIOR RETURN: THE DESTRUCTION OF THE TEMPLE

The Roman destruction of the Jerusalem Temple resulted in the exile of the Jewish community from the city, but not from the Land. It marked the end of the sacrificial ritual, its atoning and salvific symbolism, and the ecclesiastical bureaucracy of the Sadducees. The termination of the sacrificial offering yields to inner life and the service of the heart, prayer. Study and the sanctification of daily existence, the *halakhic* exercise, become a substitute for sacrifice and the splendor of the Temple. The destruction of the Jerusalem Temple started the rabbinic rebuilding that no power or political upheaval could destroy; the Temple became an inner construction.

Rabbinic theology was essentially a spiritual-social revolution that withstood the Roman Empire and created the ideological framework to face, even confront, Christianity's teaching of contempt, and the feudal system.[8]

The rabbis and teacher-commentators found a refuge in Yavneh, located on the coastal plain south of Jaffa. They reconstituted the Sanhedrin, and Yavneh was regarded the equal of Jerusalem. The biblical canon was rearranged there, and most of the rabbinic sages taught in the city. It ceased to be the center of Jewish spiritual life with the outbreak of the Bar Kokhba revolt against the Romans (132–135 CE).

Rabbinic spirituality was rooted in the Ezra-Nehemiah exploration of the biblical text and the need to actualize the covenantal relationship after the destruction of the Temple. The rabbis' task was to enlarge the Oral Torah, *Torah She ba'Al Peh,* oral *halakhic* tradition, by expounding the Written Torah, *Torah She-bikhtav,* the tradition received at Mount Sinai.[9] The expounding, commentary and explication unfolded *Halakha* as a normative criterion that guided the life of the community as a whole and each member's personal commitment.

Biblical ordinances are presented in an outlined synopsis that required an explanation. For example, Exodus 20:8–11 and Deuteronomy 5:12–15 do not detail the prohibition of working on the Sabbath. Rabbinic expounding of the text itemized what was permitted and what was not. While the *Mishnah* devotes one book, twenty-four chapters to the subject, the *Talmudim* present a phenomenology of Sabbath-spirituality in a dense volume of commentaries and explanations. Keeping dietary laws, the synagogue service of the Sabbath, family purity, are all meant to lift up everyday existence toward God, so that all of life becomes holy. Samuel H.

Dresner sums up the Sabbath provisions: "We become holy by making holy, by hallowing. We become holy by hallowing that which is not yet holy, the profane, the everyday."[10] The sanctification of daily life leads to a spirituality that translates the experience of God, the reality of the covenantal relationship, thus recreating the encounter God-Israel.

Several theological and halakhic compilations resulted from the rabbinic expounding of the biblical text. The *Siddur,* prayerbook, the *Mishnah,* halakhic interpretation of biblical law, the *Midrash,* literary interpretation of the Bible, and the two *Talmudim,* the *Jerusalem Talmud* and the *Babylonian Talmud* are examples of the rabbinic search for implementation of the word of God in daily life.

All biblical and post-biblical statutes and halakhic dispositions were codified by Maimonides (1135–1204) in his monumental *Mishne Torah.*[11] Another great code was compiled by Jacob, son of Asher Ben Yehiel, known as the *Tur,* in the fourteenth century. Rabbinic recommendations were adapted to local conditions and circumstances. Another good example of the spirituality-process is the *Shulkhan Arukh,* the Prepared Table, a code of *Halakha* compiled by Joseph Ben Ephraim Caro (1488–1575), and annotated by Moses Ben Ysrael Isserles (1520–1572), who incorporated the traditions of Eastern European Jewry.

SPIRITUALITY OF PLACE AND TIME: SYNAGOGUE AND PRAYER

As already mentioned, two of the consequences of the destruction of the Jerusalem Temple were the exile of the Jewish community from the City and the end of the sacrificial system. The exile drove the community to look for new forms of implementing the covenantal relationship. The synagogue became the center of search and evaluation of the tradition. This search set new trends for a spirituality based on prayer and the study of biblical sources.

Three times a day Jews gathered in the synagogue to pray. The schedule coincided with the sacrificial timing of the Temple. Prayer replaced sacrificial offering for the proclamation of the word, morning, afternoon and evening. Time now becomes part of the sacred endeavor. Its spirituality was and is conveyed in a symbology present in specific objects and places. The most sanctified and prominent section of the synagogue is the *Aron Ha-Kodesh,* the Ark, in which are deposited the *Sifrei-Torah,* the scrolls of the first five books of the Bible. It is always built against a wall facing Jerusalem, and indicates the direction in which the service is offered.

The perpetual light in front of the Ark, the *Ner Tamid,* recalls the light which was ever kept alight in the Tabernacle and in the Holy Temple of Jerusalem. The eternal light represents the biblical text of Proverbs 6:23, "For the Commandment is a lamp and the Torah is a light." Next in importance is the wooden platform, *Bemah,* a place in the center of the synagogue around which the worshipers have their seats, and reminiscent of the altar. From the desk that is placed thereon, the *Torah* is read and the community is led in prayer; just as the sacrifices were offered on the altar "so will we render as bullocks the words of our lips" (Hos 14:3).

Prayer as an actualization of God's Presence and covenantal relationship centers on the *Shema,* Israel's declaration of faith with its three biblical portions, Deuteronomy 6:4–9; 11:13–21, and Numbers 15:37–41. It is followed by the *Shemoneh Ezre,* eighteen and later nineteen benedictions, and the final declamation of the *Kaddish,* a sanctification of God's name, considered since medieval times a prayer for the departed and martyrs. This basic structure has been augmented by additional prayers, psalms, petitions and hymns of thanksgiving.

The *Shema* proclaims in a daily act of committed spirituality God's Unity, Israel's allegiance to the Kingdom of God, and a joyful submission to God's Commandments.

Three main ideas relate to the *Shema:* creation, revelation and redemption. The morning service starts with the prayer *Yotzer Or,* the creator of light, a thanksgiving for the creation of the light of day, and the daily renewal of creation. This concept entails the obligation for a personal commitment to the goodness of creation and the Kingdom of God.

The second prayer is the *Ahavah Rabbah,* "With abundant love have you loved us, O Lord our God, and great and overflowing tenderness have you shown to us." It is an outpouring of fervor and thanksgiving for the moral illumination bestowed upon Israel, and an affirmation of the need to live revelation in a daily life of prayer and all of life's activities.

The final concept remembered in the recitation of the *Shema* is redemption. This finds expression in three prayers of the morning service. *Emeth veyatzib,* "true and firm, established and enduring, right and faithful, beloved and precious, desirable and pleasant, revered and mighty, well ordered and acceptable, good and beautiful is this your word forever and forever." It is followed by *Al Harishonim,* "alike for former and later ages your word is good and endures forever and ever; it is true and trustworthy, an ordination which shall not pass away. True it is that you are indeed the

Lord, our God, and God of our fathers, our king, our fathers' king, our redeemer, the redeemer of our fathers, our maker, the rock of our salvation; our deliverer and rescuer from everlasting such is your name; there is no God beside you." The final hymn of thanksgiving for redemption is *Ezrath Abotenu,* praising God as the shield and savior of the community, declaring once again that God is indeed the first and the last and that "besides you we have no king, redeemer and saviour."[12]

KAVANAH AND MINHAG

The central elements renewing the spirituality of prayer are *kavanah* and *minhag. Kavanah* is considered a unique attitude that must accompany religious devotion. The Hebrew term has no exact equivalent in the English language. The original Hebrew conveys the idea of concentration, devotion, intention or inwardness, encompassing a state of oneness in devotion and inner direction toward God.

This state of mind, a preparation for prayer and commandment, is not explicitly mentioned in the Pentateuch, but is clearly referred to by the prophets. Isaiah, for instance, criticizes those who "with their mouth and with their lips do honor me, but have removed their heart far from me (29:13). Rabbinic literature, and specifically the Talmud, attaches considerable importance to *kavanah.* In T.B. *Berakot* 5, 1, it is pointed out that the early *Hasidim,* the pious ones, used to wait an hour before and after prayer to achieve a state of *kavanah* and again, to emerge from it. Later medieval authors like Maimonides rule as a matter of *Halakha* that

> since prayer without *kavanah* is not prayer at all, if one has prayed without *kavanah* he has to pray again with *kavanah.* Should one feel preoccupied or overburdened, or should one have just returned from a voyage, one must delay one's prayer till one can once again pray with *kavanah* . . . which implies freedom from all strange thoughts, and complete awareness of the fact that one stands before the Divine Presence.[13]

The *Hasidic* movement, the mystical group of Poland in the eighteenth century, was deeply concerned with the danger that prayer become mere mouthing of set words. This preoccupation was formulated by the Tzazer Rebbe who was asked by his disciples, "What does the rebbe do before praying?" "I pray," he explained, "that I may be able to pray properly."

Minhag is one of the most important bases of *Halakha.* The word is found in the Bible (2 Kgs 9:2), meaning "the driving" of a chariot, but it was taken by the rabbis to refer to "usage." It refers primarily to the customs which, having been accepted in practice, became binding and assumed the impact of *Halakha.* The word *Minhag* is also employed to designate the various liturgical rites which have developed.

Custom and usage are the natural, normal manners of expressing the contemporary experience of God, ways of conveying spirituality to ever new generations, without losing the links with tradition. *Minhag* relates the aspiration of one generation to the thoughts of the preceding ones, renewing the basic meaning of religiosity. Custom can also become an impediment, an end in itself, a ruling rather than an expression of religious experience. New forms of *Minhag* express the mood and heart of a community. For instance, the inclusion of special prayers or a time of silence at the reading of the Passover *Haggadah* to remember the Holocaust has become a way to recall missing members of the family, a missing community of six million people, a reminder of the covenantal commitment to endure evil and the realities of history. The rich spiritual experience of Sephardic Jews from Northern Africa, Greece, Italy and Southern France, and *Ashkenasim,* Jews from eastern Europe and Germany, testifies to the richness of the *Minhag* in the spirituality of the Jewish people.[14]

CREATION AND FREEDOM IN THE SPIRITUALITY OF THE SABBATH

Liturgy is a combination of word, song, and prayer, an exercise of religious commitment; it also translates a need. It is the human need for confirmation, the actualization of the Presence of God and the covenantal relationship, the encounter between person and Maker. Liturgy reenacts the primordial divine encounter, embedded in the Jewish historical experience with the world and with God.

The spirituality of liturgy is vividly expressed in four particular moments of prayer: the daily service, the celebration of the Sabbath, the redemptive power of Passover, and the renewed reckoning of the soul at Yom Kippur. Special attention will be given here to the Sabbath spirituality.

Observance and ritual are central elements in the religious life of individuals and communities. They are born out of experience of a unique moment in the human development, the meeting of God and human being.

Words and symbols become the daily remembrance of that unique experience.

The Sabbath celebration is no exception to this religious phenomenon. The reference in Genesis 2:3, "God blessed the seventh day and made it holy, because on that day he ceased from all the work he had set himself to do," is the call for inwardness and the celebration of a particular time.

The Sabbath and its spirituality go beyond the commandment of halting work, to a commemoration of creation and freedom. On Friday night, the beginning of the Sabbath in the Hebrew calendar, each ritual and liturgical expression in the community and family is charged with eschatological dimensions, reminding Jews of the covenant with God, the ethical and religious fulfillment of their witnessing, their obligations toward God, and the establishment of his Kingdom in the universe.[15]

The Hebrew Bible specifically refers to the Sabbath in two of its books, Exodus 20:8–11 and Deuteronomy 5:12–15. The latter introduces the concept of freedom from slavery that will take on a special meaning in the benediction of wine on Friday night, the *Kiddush.* Neither biblical source gives detailed rules concerning the observance of the day. The commandment is "to remember" and "to keep" the Sabbath, and to bring to a halt all work of the family and the community. The text does not indicate how to make effective in the daily experience the commandments established for the Sabbath observance. The rabbis and sages from Ezra's day to the compilation in the fifth century of the Talmud in Babylon developed a detailed account of precepts and dispositions regulating every aspect of Sabbath celebration. Their consideration covered every aspect of the life of the individual and the community, and gave to the celebration eschatological overtones that permeate every part of the Sabbath celebration.

Two central themes are remembered in the spirituality of the Sabbath, *menuhah* (rest) and freedom. The German Jewish theologian Leo Baeck implies them in the following:

> The Sabbath does not mean a mere not working, nor empty idleness. It connotes something positive. It has guided the soul into its mystery so that it is not a day that just interrupts, but a day that renews, speaks through it, of something eternal. It is the expression of the direction for life, and not just an instituted day of rest. If it were only that, or if it became that, its essence would be taken from it. It would then be only a hollow shell.[16]

Rabbi Baeck refers here to Jewish Tradition and considers the human being a partner in God's work of creation, and in bringing closer to fulfillment the divine plan for God's kingdom on earth. The *Midrash* will reflect on this particular aspect of the relationship of God and human being:

> I have placed you in this world of mine; everything I have created is for you. Set your mind to it that you do not corrupt and destroy my work.[17]

The Sabbath rest brings to a halt the creative stream of the week, but it is more than a moment of relaxation: it is a time of inner activity. The authentic expression of *menuhah,* rest, requires the individual and the community to direct their creative strength, not to the work of the world but to the spirit. The creative energies are not suspended but subjected to a transformation whose object is the inner world of the spirit. The Sabbath is a day of interiority, of self-discovery, a time to restore individual integrity, after a week of work and alienation. It allows for a recovery of self out of the routine of weekday involvement.

The liturgy speaks of a phenomenon peculiar to the Sabbath: each one receives on that day a *neshamah veterah,* an additional soul, that requires cultivation and creative self-search. It implies *nomesh,* self-change, an inner silence that transforms the self in depth and meaning. The weekday is devoted to work which for the religious person is also a creative activity; but the Sabbath is a time for inner creativity.

The *Kiddush,* the benediction over wine in the Friday night home ceremony, recalls freedom as the second basic element of the Sabbath. The blessing says that the Sabbath is "first among our sacred days," and "a remembrance of the exodus from Egypt." The Exodus narration, the liberation movement of the Jewish people as an example for all generations of humankind, relates the historical events that allowed them to continue their spiritual and religious commitment in freedom. Slavery implied subjection to a form of life that despised spirituality and the development of a religious attitude. The slavery of Egypt became symbolic of all forms of slavery, and the *Kiddush* reminds the Jew of subjection suffered throughout the centuries, from Pharaoh to contemporary antisemitism, and the devasting experience of Auschwitz.

Freedom is celebrated at home, and Jews are reminded of the creative possibilities of freedom for a religious commitment. Jews are well aware of the fact that the lack of freedom is an experience leading to spiritual suffocation and, eventually, spiritual death. It is only in an atmosphere of liberty and respect for others that a covenantal religiosity can reach high levels of inner activity and meaning.

Creative rest and freedom as elements of the Sabbath celebration have been expounded in liturgy and theological commentary for the last two thousand years. The Sabbath observance has been enriched by the liturgical experience of the Jewish people, and history has influenced its symbology and modes of commemoration. Our present time, too, requires that we rethink the meaning of the Sabbath and how to carry out its celebration, in relation to contemporary experience. What do creative energies, *menuhah,* and the sabbatical restoration of individuality in all its integrity mean to us, after the Holocaust? What is the transcendent understanding of the Sabbath in the light of the founding of the state of Israel on one hand, and the unique experience of American freedom and pluralism on the other?

THE KINGDOM OF EVIL: SPIRITUALITY AFTER AUSCHWITZ

Auschwitz was an experience of total exile, in the midst of a continent characterized by a tradition of toleration, but not of religious pluralism. It meant social and political exile, condemning a whole people to death and destruction. It was also a spiritual exile, isolating, once again, Jews and Judaism from a society inspired by two millennia of Christian presence and teaching. It was the exile of silence.

In the midst of horror—a competently organized, efficient kingdom of evil—Jews asked, are still asking, the ultimate questions about God, His Presence and Call, about the covenantal relationship. The questioning is exemplified in the daily thought of a young Jew hiding in Belgium and, eventually, gassed in Auschwitz. Moshe Flinker, a devout religious person studying the Hebrew Tradition, praying at the appointed times, in times of danger, in times of inner peace, in fear and trembling wrote:

> In olden days our ancestors thought that the climax of persecutions had been reached; but today, without swords and weapons, we see persecutions a thousand times more severe. The explanation is that today everything is highly organized.
>
> They arrange and organize, organize and arrange, until perhaps only one in a thousand is able to flee or hide. And why can they now organize everything in a manner that was not previously possible? The reason is . . . that with the Germans everything is official, everything is

> done according to the law. The law condemns us. Just as there is a law against stealing, so there is a law to persecute the Jews. . . .
>
> So we thus see that there really is a difference between our sufferings since our exile and our anguish in these terrible times. Why does the Lord not prevent this, or, on the other hand, why does He permit our tormentors to persecute us? And what can be the result of these persecutions?[18]

But young Moshe is confident; he trusts in a tradition of covenantal hope; he knows of the ultimate victory of hope. He writes in his diary:

> The victor in this war that we are living through will not be either of the opposing sides, but God; not England and not America, but the Lord of Israel will triumph. . . . Obviously my outlook is a religious one. I hope to be excused for this, for had I not religion, I would never find any answer at all to the problems that confront me.[19]

The problems, however, remain and are the quest of a people that within one generation has known death and revival, the Holocaust and the founding of the state of Israel. The questioning touches on the very foundation of being Jewish: What is the significance of God after this experience? What is the meaning of being chosen, of belonging to a people with a vocation? How can prayer portray the Holocaust desolation, the broken heart of Israel? Can the spirituality of centuries, the meeting with God as portrayed by Tradition, have any transcendent meaning today?

The temptations are many: to negate God, and religious commitment, to renounce spiritual witnessing, to abandon millennia of spirituality and religiosity, conceding a posthumous victory to the totalitarian paganism of Nazism. The temptation is to remain in exile . . .

The challenge to Jewish faith and *Halakha,* living and implementing God's revelation, has never been so overwhelming, so devastating. Hope, the grounding element of Jewish existence, however, is equally present, hope in renewal, in a new *Halakha,* a way and means to respond to the exile of Auschwitz, hope in hope. Young Moshe described this search, in commitment to the survival of Israel and the new dimensions of Jewish vocation, in a prayer written before his deportation, summing up Jewish spirituality, the centrality of God, and our present search:

> Before us tread/with sacred flags/our heroes to be killed/And above us the heroes of our forefathers/The land our land!/We are here.
>
> God of my people/God of my spirit/My God/Thou art my

rock/my fortress/For Thee I yearn/And will continue to yearn/My God, my God/The God of my people/My God, my God/O God/In what manner/Could I praise Thee/In what manner/Could I embrace Thee/My God, my God/O God/I am your servant/And Thou art my God/O God/My rock and my fortress/Thee shall I worship/In awe and terror/Thee and Thy people/My beloved people/My God, my God/The God of my people/My God, my God.[20]

NOTES

1. Franz Rosenzweig, *The Star of Redemption* (New York: Holt, Rinehart & Winston, 1971). Ronald H. Miller, "The Spirituality of Franz Rosenzweig," in Matthew Fox, ed., *Western Spirituality: Historical Roots, Ecumenical Routes* (Notre Dame: Fides/Claretian, 1979).

2. Rudolf Otto, *The Idea of the Holy* (New York: Oxford University Press, 1958).

3. Joseph Elias, ed., *The Haggadah* (New York: Mesorah Publications, 1977). Lawrence A. Hoffmann, *The Canonization of the Synagogue Service* (Notre Dame: University of Notre Dame Press, 1979), Chapter 1, "The Passover Haggadah."

4. Meir Zlotowitz, ed., *Megillas Eichah, Lamentations* (New York: Art Scroll Studios, 1976). Isaac Klein, *A Guide to Jewish Religious Practice* (New York: Jewish Theological Seminary of America, 1979).

5. Yeheskel Kaufmann, *The Babylonian Captivity and Deutero-Isaiah* (New York: Union of American Hebrew Congregations, 1970). Ralph W. Klein, *Israel in Exile* (Philadelphia: Fortress Press, 1979).

6. Simon Rawidowicz, "An Interpretation," in *Proceedings of the American Academy for Jewish Research,* Vol. XXVI, New York, 1957, p. 85.

7. *Ibid.,* pp. 85f.

8. Ellis Rivkin, *A Hidden Revolution* (Nashville: Abingdon, 1978).

9. Harry C. Schimmel, *The Oral Law* (New York: Feldheim Publishers, 1971).

10. Samuel H. Dresner and Seymour Siegel, *The Jewish Dietary Laws* (New York: Burning Bush Press, 1966), p. 18.

11. Parts of the Maimonides Code were translated into English and published by Yale University Press in its Yale Judaica Series.

12. A.Z. Idelsohn, *Jewish Liturgy and Its Development* (New York: Sacred Music Press. Hebrew Union College-Jewish Institute of Religion, 1932). Jakob J. Petuchowski, *Understanding Jewish Prayer* (New York: Ktav Publishing, 1972).

13. Maimonides, *Mishneh Torah. The Book of Adoration* (New York, Jerusalem: Boys Town Publishers, 1965), Section: Prayer, 4, 15, 16.

14. Abraham Chill, *The Minhagim.* The Customs and Ceremonies of Judaism. Their Origins and Rationale (New York: Sepher-Hermon Press, 1979).

15. Solomon Goldman, *A Guide to the Sabbath* (London: Jewish Chronicle Publications, 1961).

16. Leo Baeck, *This People Israel: The Meaning of Jewish Existence* (Philadelphia: Jewish Publications Society of America, 1965), p. 137.

17. H. Freedman and Maurice Simon, eds., *The Midrash,* Vol. VIII, Ecclesiastes (London: Soncino Press, 1961).

18. Moshe Flinker, *Young Moshe's Diary.* The Spiritual Torment of a Jewish Boy in Nazi Europe (Jerusalem: Yad Vashem, 1965), p. 28.

19. *Ibid.,* p. 30.

20. *Ibid.,* p. 114.

2. The Meaning of Christian Spirituality

Margaret Mary Kelleher

1. ANTHROPOLOGICAL FOUNDATIONS

A discussion of the meaning of Christian spirituality must begin with a clarification of what is intended by the use of the term "spirituality" since this word has acquired a certain degree of ambiguity. The understanding proposed in this article is that spirituality refers to and is a reflection upon the experience of the dynamic interaction which occurs between the human spirit and the Holy Spirit in any given human life. The implicit anthropology, or theory of the nature of the human person which provides the foundations for such an understanding, is one which regards the human person as essentially open to transcendence and capable of the experience of self-transcendence.

Bernard Lonergan is one who has developed such an anthropology as the foundation for the rest of his work, and his theory of the human subject is quite appropriate for use in spirituality because it offers a way of speaking about the development of the life of the spirit in which all of the operations of the individual can be integrated.[1] His theory rests on the claim that an orientation to self-transcendence constitutes the basic structure of the human person. This single intending toward self-transcendence is in fact the playing out of two unrestricted desires: the desire to know and the desire to love. Those desires are the operators which lead an individual through various levels of consciousness toward the goal of authenticity which is achieved to the degree that a person is attentive, intelligent, reasonable, responsible, and loving.

The desires to know and love become explicit in questions which promote understanding, judgment, decisions and actions. Each new type of question brings the person to a higher level of consciousness, but the level from which the individual moves is incorporated into and fulfilled within the new level.[2] This integration of lower levels within the higher overcomes the dualism between body and spirit which has often been associated with Christian spirituality. The human spirit is incarnate and can achieve authenticity only in and through the body. The orientation of the human spirit to self-transcendence which begins on the sensitive level and moves through the intellectual, rational and responsible levels of consciousness is fulfilled when the person operates out of a fifth level as one who lives in a dynamic state of being-in-love without restriction.[3]

Although the desire for self-transcendence in knowledge and love is potentially unrestricted it must work itself out in a dialectical opposition with the conflicting desire for self-enclosure which appears in the urge to flee from understanding, resist the truth, escape from responsibility and run from love.[4] It is also limited in fact by the boundary or horizon within which the individual operates.[5] This horizon is the outer limit of one's vision of oneself and of reality. It is the product of such factors as genetic makeup, family background, education, psychological type, choices made, gifts and opportunities received, etc., and it controls further development by setting the limits for the kinds of questions one asks. New horizons allow new questions about experience and this leads to new ways of understanding, new judgments, different decisions, and transformed ways of acting. However, the establishment of a new horizon happens in response to a call or gift and only through the destruction or breaking through of the old one. This transformation of horizon and the establishment of a new world of meaning is identified by Lonergan as the experience of a conversion, and he specifies three different types: intellectual, moral, and religious.[6]

Whenever a conversion occurs, the desire for self-transcendence in knowledge and love is liberated from the restriction of one horizon and allowed to flourish within a more expansive horizon. In a religious conversion God's love becomes one's horizon, and this new horizon makes its appearance in transformed feelings, understandings, judgments, decisions, and actions. The gift of God's love shatters the boundaries of the previous horizon and releases the desire to love. This human desire for self-transcendence is the life of the human spirit, and the life of any individual can be understood as a dynamic interaction between the desire of the human spirit and the attraction of the Holy Spirit, the boundless horizon.

The existence of a new horizon can be recognized by the transformation of feelings which occurs in the individual. It may appear in the feeling of peace which replaces anxiety and fear, in the hope which goes beyond despair, in the feeling of acceptance which transforms the guilt, in the love which overcomes alienation. These transformed feelings are the sign that new values, new meanings, have been recognized and appropriated by the person or persons concerned. The objects, words, or people acting as carriers of these new meanings become symbols of the transformed values and play an important role in enabling the individuals who have entered the new horizon to periodically remember and reappropriate those values. The new feelings promote the desire for self-transcendence and can become major factors in orienting the lives of those involved, in shaping their horizons.[7]

Since a person's horizon sets the outer limit of his or her self-image and perception of reality, the liberation of the desire for self-transcendence within a new and expanded horizon is accompanied by the corresponding development of a new self-image. The expansion of one's horizon allows the imagination to detect new possibilities in the data of experience, and it is as if the person sees with new eyes, experiences a transformed vision. Communities form when individuals who have had similar experiences of transformation and share the new vision come to recognize themselves as living within the same horizon of meaning. The meanings which constitute the new image of themselves and their new vision of reality will be carried in and communicated by the art, symbols, language and lives of the persons involved.[8]

2. JESUS' JOURNEY OF TRANSFORMATION

In accord with this fundamental anthropology which describes human life as an ongoing process of self-transcendence in knowledge and love, Christian spirituality can be understood as a horizon of meaning shared by those who have come to interpret their own experience of transformation as a participation in the meaning of the transforming event of the life, death, and resurrection of Jesus Christ. Those who wish to explore the meaning of Christian spirituality must attend to the writings of the earliest Christian communities in order to discover what these people identified as the carriers of Jesus' meaning. The message and deeds of Jesus which are recorded there can provide us with a way of entering the early Christian world of meaning and discovering what they understood to be the factors which shaped Jesus' horizon and thus their own.

a. Jesus' Jewish Spirituality

In his book, *Jesus,* Edward Schillebeeckx calls our attention to the fact that Jesus' own spirituality was first of all Jewish.[9] He lived in a world of meaning shaped by the literature of the different Jewish traditions, and his piety was formed in relation to the principles, hopes, and promises which he found there. Any awareness Jesus had of himself as a prophet and any such understanding on the part of his followers must be interpreted within the context of the writings of the prophetic tradition. Besides the Jewish tradition and piety in which he had been raised, there were other major factors in his experience which were seen by the early Christians as carriers of his meaning. Those who wrote the Gospels present a picture of Jesus as one whose horizon was further shaped by the Spirit who anointed him at his baptism in the Jordan and led him on his journey, by the word he heard from the One he called "Abba," by the kingdom he preached in word and deed, and by the cross to which his journey led.

b. Baptism of Jesus

The baptism of Jesus was of major significance for the early Christians who eventually came to see it as a prototype of their own baptism. In each of the accounts of Jesus' baptism reference is made to the descent of the Spirit upon him. The story as told in the Gospel according to Luke is as follows:

> During a general baptism of the people, when Jesus too had been baptized and was praying, heaven opened and the Holy Spirit descended on him in bodily form like a dove; and there came a voice from heaven, "Thou art my Son, my Beloved; on thee my favor rests" (Lk 3:21–22).

Although there is no explicit reference to an anointing of Jesus in this passage or in the other Gospel accounts of the baptism, other references suggest that the Church came to understand this event as the occasion on which Jesus was anointed by the Spirit as prophet, as Christos-Messiah.[10] In Acts 10:38 Jesus is referred to as the one whom "God anointed with the Holy Spirit and with power," and in Luke 4:18 Jesus is depicted as applying the anointing mentioned in Isaiah 61:1–2 to himself. Schillebeeckx presents Jesus' baptism as a disclosure experience for Jesus himself and as Jesus' first appearance as a prophet, one in which he reaffirmed John the Baptist's summons to the people to return to God and let their hearts be transformed.[11] The fact that Jesus was anointed with the spirit of sonship established him as the prophet whose message came from an intimate relationship with God.[12]

c. Jesus' Relationship with God

The foundation of Jesus' intimate relationship with God is to be found in the unique way in which the word or self-communication of God appeared in Jesus.[13] The Gospels portray Jesus as one driven by an overwhelming desire to hear and live the word of God, as one in whom this Word became flesh (Jn 1:14). Jesus is depicted as one who is led and empowered by the Spirit to become the hearer par excellence of God's word. His followers eventually came to see in him the embodiment of the new covenant, the new relationship which God had promised to his people through the prophet Jeremiah (Jer 31:31–34). The relationship is described by the prophet as one in which God's people will respond in fidelity to the law which is written on their hearts, one in which they will be led to an intimate knowledge of God. They will be able to hear the word and respond because they will have been made new by the experience of God's forgiveness and the gift of his spirit. The prophet Ezekiel describes the experience in this way:

> I will give you a new heart and place a new spirit within you. I will take the heart of stone from your body and give you a heart of flesh. I will put my spirit into you and make you conform to my statutes, keep my laws and live by them . . . you shall become my people and I will become your God (36:26–28).

This biblical description of conversion as a transformation of the heart by the gift of a new spirit is the promise of the creation of a new horizon, a new identity. The notion that the gift of God's Spirit will be experienced as a new creation is developed in the writings of Deutero-Isaiah, and the qualities of the transformed persons and the new relationship are described by this tradition in the four servant songs (Is 42:1–4; 49:1–7; 50:4–11; 52:13—53:12). The servant is depicted as one whose ears have been opened so that he might hear the word of God, one who obeys that word even in the face of persecution, one who never ceases to trust in the One who speaks the word. The foundation for such an ability to hear and live the word, to trust even in suffering, is found in the intimate relationship between the servant and Yahweh, a relationship which is transformative. The early Christians came to see Jesus as the embodiment of this transformation, as the new creature who lived in such intimacy with God that he could hear and faithfully live the message of God.

The word which appears in the Gospels and letters of the early Christian communities as the symbol of the intimate relationship which existed between Jesus and God is "Abba," the word used by Jesus when he addressed God, one which can be translated as "dear Father," "my Father." Joachim Jeremias suggests that this intimate form of address expressed the heart of the revelation granted to Jesus by God and that it was the foundation of his mission and authority.[14] Schillebeeckx identifies Jesus' Abba experience as "the soul, source and ground of Jesus' message, praxis and ministry," as the religious experience which enabled Jesus to proclaim his message of hope.[15] He sees Jesus' use of Abba as an expression of the heart of his spirituality, the desire to discover and do the Father's will.[16] In accord with the understanding of horizon as the outer limit or boundary in relation to which one shapes his or her identity, we can say that Jesus' life and self-image were shaped in relation to a horizon which he knew in a personal and intimate way, one which he addressed as Father. In his ministry we see one who lived within the horizon of God's love, one in whom God's Spirit operated.

d. Jesus and the Kingdom

The word which Jesus heard from his Father he then proclaimed to his people in the message that the kingdom, or God's rule, was at hand. In proclaiming the nearness of the kingdom, Jesus was announcing God's desire for the salvation of all people, his limitless mercy.[17] The meaning of Jesus' proclamation of the coming of the kingdom is to be found in the way he lived, in the parables he told, and in those he enacted. The God of these parables is one who is merciful, forgiving, compassionate and faithful, one who calls upon human beings to respond to his love by changing their ways and beginning to live according to the values of the kingdom. The stories which tell of Jesus' healing those sick in mind and body depict him living the message of the nearness of the kingdom, the message that God is concerned about human beings in their suffering. The reality of the kingdom became present in the actions of Jesus.

Perhaps the Gospel stories which most adequately reveal the meaning of Jesus' message that the kingdom was at hand are those which portray him at meals.[18] A reading of the Gospels makes it clear how central a factor the meals Jesus shared with others was in carrying and communicating his meaning within the early Christian communities. There are stories of Jesus eating with sinners and with the outcasts of society (e.g., Lk 7:36–47; Mk 2:15–17) and, in doing so, extending God's invitation to all to come and enter into communion. Other stories tell of Jesus acting as host and providing bountiful meals for those who followed him (e.g., Mk 6:34–44; 8:1–9) and thereby disclosing the bounteous nature of God's generosity. The Gospels also describe an intimate meal of farewell shared by Jesus with his disciples before the passion, and they tell of those disciples who later recognized the presence of their risen Lord in the context of a meal (Lk 24:28–31; Jn 21:12–13). The invitation to come and share a meal with Jesus was an invitation to say yes to the coming of the kingdom, to hope in the bountiful goodness and compassion of God, to believe that death is not the end of the journey.

e. Jesus and the Cross

The journey on which Jesus set out after being anointed and empowered by the Spirit, the word which he was able to hear, and the kingdom which he lived and preached all led to the cross, and any Christian spirituality which is authentic has to face and accept this reality. The cross is the place where the message of Jesus is tested, for it seems to negate any reason for trusting in the One he called Father. Yet the cross is also the logical outcome, the ultimate self-giving for the one whose whole life was lived in God's Spirit. Jesus, who heard and spoke the word of God during his life, also spoke that word on the cross. He proclaimed there the truth that living in the horizon of God's love means trusting in that love in and through death, and he established the principle that anyone who wished to follow him on his journey of transformation would achieve self-transcendence only in and through the acceptance of death.

The symbolic action of drinking from the cup is placed in association with Jesus' death in the literature of the first Christians. The accounts of Jesus in the garden of Gethsemane portray him referring to his forthcoming passion in terms of drinking from the cup, and they also make it clear that the cup was seen in association with the will of his Father (Mt 26:36–44; Mk 14:35–36; Lk 22:41–42; Jn 18:11). In the accounts of the Last Supper the cup appears both as a symbol of death—the blood of Jesus poured out—and as a symbol of hope, seen in the promise that there will be a future time when Jesus will drink from the cup anew in the kingdom of God (Mt 26:26–29; Mk 14:23–25; Lk 32:17–19). Schillebeeckx sees the fact that Jesus, in the face of death, continued to offer the cup to his disciples to be a sign of Jesus' hope and conviction of the power of God even over death.[19] He suggests that in this action Jesus may have been inviting his friends to a fellowship with him which he believed was stronger than death.[20]

f. Jesus—The Risen One

The faith of Christians rests in the fact that Jesus' journey did not end in death, but that he was led through death to a new life and made himself known to those who had been his disciples in such a way that they came to proclaim that God had raised him from the dead (1 Thes 1:10). Jesus' trust in the One he called Father was vindicated and proclaimed in the confession of the early Christians that God, by his power, had brought the crucified One to life again.[21] God's Spirit, which had anointed Jesus at his baptism and which had led him on his journey to the cross, broke through the barrier of death and opened up a new eschatological horizon of hope for all who would come to believe in Jesus of Nazareth as the Christ, the one anointed and totally filled with God's Spirit.

3. PARTICIPATING IN THE HORIZON OF JESUS

The spirituality of those who first came to accept Jesus as the Christ, whose own journey of transformation was made in response to the invitation and direction of his Spirit, was naturally influenced by those factors which had shaped Jesus' horizon. The meanings they appropriated from his own life and the subsequent development of these meanings can be discovered by exploring the language, art, ritual, and lives of those who have called themselves Christians. The totality of the meaning will not be found in any one thing or one tradition, for the exigencies of history and the reality of cultural differences also act as forces which shape the horizon of Christian meaning for individuals and communities. Just as Jesus interpreted his experience of the Spirit in relation to his Jewish traditions, those who came after him would use the language and ideas available to them in their particular milieus to interpret their experience. The challenge is to discover those values and meanings which are constant, which have been carried and communicated in various ways throughout history. The place to begin, of course, is with the experience of those who first came to believe in Jesus as the Lord and Christ, those who made up the first Christian communities. Their experience and understanding of what it meant to share in Jesus' own horizon of meaning can provide some of the criteria for judging the authenticity of later interpretations.

a. A Process of Transformation

A reading of the literature of the early Christian communities will substantiate the description of the Christian spiritual life as a process of transformation mediated by the word, the light, water, the spirit, the table, and the cross. Christians are those persons whose desire for God has been activated by the word which invites them to come out of the darkness and into the light, those who respond and come to quench their thirst and be reborn in the waters of new life where they are anointed by the Spirit, those who are led to the table of fellowship where they recognize Jesus in the breaking of the bread, and where they are reminded that in taking the cup they say "yes" to the cross and proclaim their hope in the ongoing transformation of themselves and their world. All of these elements of Christian spirituality can be gathered from the descriptions of life in the earliest communities. Initiation into these communities was a process of conversion. We do not know the explicit shape of the process in different communities, but it has been described in general by Aidan Kavanagh as a "Spirit-laden process" which began with the proclamation of the Gospel, led to conversion, and was consummated in a water bath which led the individual into full participation in the life of a Spirit-filled community.[22]

b. Called by the Word

The first step in the conversion process was the proclamation of the word, the good news that Jesus had been made Lord and Christ, and that all were invited to share in his life, the life of the Spirit. In the Jewish tradition it was the word of God spoken through the prophets which gathered the people into assemblies. The first Christians came to recognize Jesus, the one who had heard, spoken and lived God's word, as the one who had gathered them into the assembly of the new covenant. Those who were enabled to recognize him as alive after his death proclaimed this good news to others, and this was the beginning of the new community which gathered in his name. Those who came to believe in Jesus as the risen Lord and Christ then proclaimed the good news of salvation to others in his name.

After his conversion, Paul understood himself to be "set apart for the service of the Gospel" (Rom 1:1), one he describes in this way.

> This gospel God announced beforehand in sacred scriptures through his prophets. It is about his Son: on the human level he was born of David's stock, but on the level of the spirit—the Holy Spirit—he was declared Son of God by a mighty act in that he rose from the dead: it is about Jesus Christ our Lord (Rom 1:2–4).

In the First Letter of Peter, the Christians are told that they have been born anew through the living and enduring word of God, the word of the Gospel preached to them (1 Pet 1:23–25). Before the Gospels were ever put together in their present literary form they were orally proclaimed. The stories gathered there were part of an oral tradition which told of the good news of Jesus Christ so that others might believe in him. The Fourth Gospel as we have it now identifies Jesus as the Word of God (Jn 1:14), the Word who can give eternal life (Jn 5:24–26). One who hears the word always has to make a decision in terms of response, and the author of the Fourth Gospel has Jesus telling the people that a refusal to let his word find a home in them is a refusal of life (5:38–40). The following passage from the First Letter of John is an excellent example of the foundational nature of the Word for a Christian spirituality.

> It was there from the beginning; we have heard it; we have seen it with our own eyes; we looked upon it, and felt it with our own hands; and it is of this we tell. Our theme is the word of life. This life was made visible; we have seen it and bear our testimony; we here declare to you the eternal life which dwelt with the Father and was made visible to us. What we have seen and heard we declare to you, so that you and we together may share in a common life, that life which we share with the Father and his Son Jesus Christ (1 Jn 1:1–4).

c. Led to the Water

Those who heard the word of life and were enabled to respond by the Spirit were led to the waters of baptism where they were baptized in the name of Jesus Christ and made members of the community of the Spirit. The early Church associated water with Jesus and the Spirit, and this is made clear in the Fourth Gospel where Jesus is proclaimed as the one who can give the water of eternal life to those who thirst, living water which is the life of the Spirit (Jn 4:1–15; 7:37–39). It is in the same Gospel that Jesus tells Nicodemus that a new birth by water and the spirit is required for entrance into the kingdom (Jn 3:5–7). The association of the symbolism of water with the life of the Spirit of Jesus which was made by the early Christians is clearly evident in the vision of the New Jerusalem which is portrayed in the Book of Revelation. There the river of the water of life is pictured as flowing from the throne of God and the Lamb through the middle of the city, enabling trees to grow which produce fruit and leaves which can serve for the healing of the nations. The book ends with an invitation to all who are thirsty, who desire this water of life, to come and accept the free gift (Rev 22:1–3, 17).

d. Brought into Light

The process of conversion which began with the proclamation of the word of the Gospel and led to the waters of baptism was one of struggle, one in which sin had to be overcome in order that the person could see and walk in the light of Christ. This is described in the Gospels and letters of the early Christians as a process of being enabled to see, a transformation of blindness, the experience of a new vision. In the Fourth Gospel, Jesus is portrayed as the light which has never been mastered by the darkness (1:5), as the light of the world who will not let his followers wander in the dark (8:12) but who will cure them of their blindness and enable them to see him and believe in his message (9:1–41). The light of Jesus created a new horizon which led people to see him and themselves in a new way. The three accounts of Paul's conversion in the Acts of the Apostles (9:1–27; 22:1–21; 26:19–23) all use light symbolism and speak of Paul "seeing Jesus," a seeing which Schillebeeckx portrays as a "Christological seeing," an understanding of Jesus as the Christ, one made possible by grace alone.[23] As the following passage indicates, the conversion process of all those who came to believe in the risen Jesus was understood as a process of coming into the light, one of illumination.

> For though you were once all darkness, now as Christians you are light. Live like men who are at home in daylight, for where light is, there all goodness springs up, all justice and truth. Try to find out what would please the Lord; take no part in the barren deeds of darkness, but show them up for what they are (Eph 5:7–11).

e. Gathered at the Table

The process of hearing the word, receiving the waters of life, and coming into the light of Christ was one which led the person into the community that had gathered in his name. Acts 2:42–47 is an important source for discovering the characteristics of those communities which gathered in Jerusalem. These verses comprise the first of several major summaries to be found in the Acts of the Apostles, and they present a description of ideal Christian community life. Verse 46 speaks of the Christians "attending the temple together and breaking bread in their homes," reflecting a stage in which these early Christians understood themselves to be both intimately related to the Jewish traditions and in the process of developing a consciousness of themselves as a new assembly gathered by Christ. "The breaking of the bread" was one of the earliest names for the celebration of the Eucharist, but it was not the only thing that happened when the assembly gathered. The accounts in the Acts of the Apostles tell us that the apostles taught (2:42), that there was common prayer (4:24–30), and that material goods were pooled and distributed according to need (2:44–46). Breaking the bread and sharing it with one another had to be accompanied by a sharing of other goods as well.

From the description of the churches or assemblies given in Acts and in the letters of Paul it is clear that there was no uniform model. The structure and identity of each was shaped in relation to each situation. The heritage that belonged to the Christians in Jerusalem because they were Jews was not a part of the horizon of the community at Corinth. There were bound to be some differences in the way they structured their assemblies and expressed the message of the Gospel. In both communities, however, the centrality of gathering at the table is clearly evident. Paul does much in his letters to the Corinthians to explicate the meaning of this action.

Paul uses the Greek word *koinonia* to refer to the relationship with Christ to which Christians are called (1 Cor 1:9). In his study of the meaning of this word, Michael McDermott has pointed out the fact that Paul took this secular Greek word meaning "common share or participation in" and usually designating a union of ideas based on common interest or friendship, and used it in a way which would suggest that Christians share or participate in Jesus Christ.[24] Paul's use of the word indicates the fact that the experience of Christian union and salvation is based not on the sharing of a thing but in a relationship which involves the Christian in an intimate union with the Father, one which occurs through Christ and is mediated by the Holy Spirit.[25]

f. A Gift To Be Shared

Koinonia is first of all the gift of a relationship with the Father, in Christ, through the Spirit, but as a result of this gift of God the recipients experience *koinonia* with one another.[26] This communion, which is initially given, must be actively realized, however, by the members of the community.[27] The dynamic sense of *koinonia* is related to Paul's second use of the word to mean a "thing to be participated in," and the "thing" he means is the sufferings of the other members of the community. The obligation of the community to share in one another's suffering and to attempt to alleviate it arises from the fact that each of them shares in the redemptive suffering of Christ.[28]

The most complete expression of the fellowship (*koinonia*) established by baptism, and the best opportunity for further deepening this union, occurred when the community came to the table to celebrate the Eucharist, the communion (*koinonia*) in the body and blood of Christ. Paul expressed this when he wrote to the Corinthians:

> The cup of blessing which we bless, is it not a participation (*koinonia*) in the blood of Christ? The bread which we break, is it not a participation (*koinonia*) in the body of Christ (1 Cor 10:16)?

The communion experienced by those who share in the bread and cup is grounded in the experience of sharing in something greater than themselves, in being part of a body. Those who received the body and blood of Christ in the Lord's Supper became the body of Christ, and an authentic celebration of the Lord's Supper required a corresponding participation in the attitude of self-giving which had governed Christ's life and death. The *koinonia* expressed in the sharing of a meal with the risen Lord was also to be expressed in the assembly, in the unity of the participants, in the sharing of one another's sufferings, and in a sharing of goods with the poor. Paul makes it clear to the Corinthians that anything less than this is an unworthy celebration, a negation of the Lord's Supper, and a cause for bringing judgment upon themselves (1 Cor 11:17–18, 20, 27, 29).

The spiritual life of the first Christians as described by them in their own writings was understood as a gift, but one which carried with it serious consequences. The gift consisted in the fact that they had been anointed in baptism with the Spirit of Jesus. The task which accompanied the gift was that they learn from and dwell in that Spirit (1 Jn 2:26–27). In his letters, Paul speaks of this life in the Spirit as a "new creation," the qualities of which will appear in the love, joy, peace, patience, kindness, goodness, fidelity, gentleness and self-control of those who let the Spirit which is the source of their life direct its course (Gal 5:22; 6:16). He sees the one Holy Spirit as the source both of the unity of the Christian community and of the varied gifts given to individuals to be used in building up the body (1 Cor 12:1–13; 14:27). He tells the community at Rome that because they share in Jesus' Spirit they too are able to call God "Abba, Father" and should live in the hope engendered by that kind of intimate relationship (Rom 8:14–15, 23–25).

Paul never lets the communities forget the fact that the new creation came only through death on the cross, and that being led by the Spirit of Jesus means sharing in his suffering. However, the message of the cross is always set within the context of hope; the proclamation is always one which claims that in the midst of death, life will be revealed and will triumph.

> Wherever we go we carry death with us in our body, the death that Jesus died, that in this body also life may reveal itself, the life that Jesus lives. . . . We know that he who raised the Lord Jesus to life will with Jesus raise us too and bring us to his presence and you with us (2 Cor 4:10, 14).

4. SYMBOLIC CARRIERS OF CHRISTIAN MEANING

The literature of the first Christian churches has allowed us to identify the following symbols as carriers of the meaning of their spirituality: the word, light, water, the table, and the cross. All of these were essential dimensions of the conversion process through which people who were led by the Spirit became identified as Christians. All were understood within the horizon of meaning created by Jesus' own experience and, as part of this horizon, they shape the identity or self-image of all who come to see in Jesus both the revelation of God's love and the image of what a human person can become if the Spirit is allowed to permeate the human operations of consciousness. These symbols still carry essential meanings for those who call themselves Christian, but a complete history of what Christian communities have done with regard to each of these would reveal interesting changes in the self-understanding of those communities. Indications of the role played by these symbols in Christian spirituality will be given in what follows.

a. Word

The belief that God speaks a word to human persons, one which they are capable of hearing, is the foundation of the relationship which is at the heart of a spiritual life and of the life of prayer in which this relationship is played out. The desire to know and love God which structures the spirit of each person searches for a word of encouragement, a word of revelation from the One desired. Prayer is a process of waiting for and attending to that word, and then engaging in dialogue with the One who speaks. Those who engage in prayer, who listen in order that they may hear the word, must become sensitive to the varied ways in which the word is spoken. God has spoken his word in creation, he has spoken through his prophets, and he has made his word incarnate in Jesus Christ. There is no person or situation in life excluded from the possibility of being a carrier of his word.

The recognition of the fact that those who hear God's word can then speak it to one another is the foundation of communities which have gathered in the name of the Lord and of the ministries performed by the members of such groups. The Scriptures we have are examples of the word of God spoken through human persons, and they occupy a position of priority among all possible sources for hearing this word. Throughout the history of the Church the Scriptures have provided source material for individual and communal prayer. In the early Church the proclamation of the eucharistic prayer of thanksgiving was understood to be a ministry of the word, a prophetic act. There was no dichotomy between word and sacrament in the early centuries of the Church because the sacramental actions were understood as non-verbal proclamations of the word.[29]

As the Church grew and developed and more efforts were made to interpret its experience there emerged a number of different ways of understanding the role of the word and therefore of its place in the ministry of the Church. It could be seen as a word of illumination, one of revelation, one of nourishment, of healing, of instruction. An unfortunate development in the medieval period was the fact that the word in relation to the sacraments received more emphasis as an instrument in the hands of the minister than as an effective word of proclamation in its own right. This emphasis on the instrumentality of the minister's word was accompanied by a lack of attention to the word of the Scriptures and led to a split between word and sacrament which called for reform. In his efforts at reform Martin Luther taught that preaching of the word and celebration of the sacrament were both necessary for a true Christian community, and he and his followers attempted to restore the primacy of the word. The emphasis of these and other reformers on the primacy of the word and the fact that the fathers at the Council of Trent did little to relate the word and the Eucharist only hardened a word/sacrament polarity and led to the unfortunate development of emphasis being given to one at the expense of the other in the different communities within the Church. Developments in the twentieth century have done a great deal to restore the integral relationship between the word as preached and the word enacted. A characteristic of contemporary Christian spirituality is the fact that people are rediscovering the power of the word in their lives and are seeking ways of becoming sensitive to that word. They are rediscovering the truth of what Johann Arndt wrote in the seventeenth century in his book on *True Christianity.*

> Since God's Word is the seed of God in us, it must bring forth spiritual fruit and it must do so through faith in the manner taught and testified externally in the Scriptures or it is a dead seed and a dead birth. What the Scripture teaches I must experience for my comfort in spirit and faith. God did not reveal the Holy Scriptures so that they might externally on paper remain a dead letter, but that they might become living in us in spirit and faith and that a completely new inner man might arise.[30]

b. Light

Light and its associated imagery has been employed by Christians from the earliest days as a way of capturing and communicating dimensions of their spiritual experience. One of the earliest names for baptism itself was "illumination" or "enlightenment" as Justin explains in the defense of the Christian faith which he addressed to the Roman emperor around 160 (CE):

> This washing is called enlightenment, because those that are experiencing these things have their minds enlightened.[31]

In a fourth century classic written by Gregory of Nyssa entitled *The Life of Moses,* the spiritual life is portrayed as a journey, an ongoing process of transformation in which one is led by the Holy Spirit who is portrayed as fire, cloud, and light. The end of the journey is achieved when one attains true knowledge described as "a seeing that consists in not seeing," an experience of penetrating the "luminous darkness."[32] The opposition of light and darkness or the description of a darkness which is really light is typical of the language used by some mystics to carry something of the meaning of their experience.

An example of one who used the images of fire and light to speak of his experience is the Eastern Christian mystic St. Symeon the New Theologian who died in 1022. His emphasis on the operations of the Holy Spirit was unique for his time, and he was noted for his use of the image of light to describe the growth of mystical union with Jesus Christ.[33] He explained that the Holy Spirit was given in baptism, but that the gift was deepened throughout one's life in an ongoing baptism of the Spirit. He speaks of God as completely imcomprehensible but as One who gives us his light which stimulates a flame of divine desire and enables the person to see in the darkness.[34] The Christian life is described by Symeon as a process of deification or theosis, one in which persons are transformed by the Holy Spirit to become sons of God as Christ is by nature.[35] He makes it clear that asceticism on the part of the person is a necessary condition for seeing the inner light.

Light has been used as the image of love and desire by the sixteenth century Spanish mystic John of the Cross. The first three stanzas of his poem "The Dark Night" are as follows:

> One dark night,
> Fired with love's urgent longing
> —Ah, the sheer grace!—
> I went out unseen,
> My house being now all stilled;
>
> In darkness and secure,
> By the secret ladder, disguised,
> —Ah, the sheer grace!—
> In darkness and concealment,
> My house being now all stilled;
>
> On that glad night,
> In secret, for no one saw me,
> Nor did I look at anything,
> With no other light or guide
> Than the one that burned in my heart.[36]

In verse one it is clear that the fire which is leading the soul on is loving desire, and verse three tells us that it is that same loving desire which serves as the light on the journey. The desire or light entices and supports the individual through the journey into the dark night. In his commentary John explains that this fire of love is not felt at the outset but that as it increases the soul becomes aware of being attracted and enkindled by the love of God.[37] He goes on to explain that the divine light which comes to a soul not yet illumined causes spiritual darkness both because it surpasses the capacity of the soul and because it exposes the darkness and sinfulness of the individual.[38] True illumination comes only at the end of a period of purgation, and he uses the image of a log being transformed by fire to describe the transformation of the person who is brought into the light.[39] The fire of love is a passionate desire for union with God, and it is this love alone which guides the person through the night of transformation to union with God. John also uses the images of the "living flame" and the "lamp of love" in his poem "The Living Flame of Love" and in his commentary explains that the flame of love, the fire, is the Holy Spirit which consumes, transforms, and refreshes the soul.[40] Once again, he explains that the flame brings the soul's infirmities to light, but that once these are healed the person "is illumined, and being transformed, beholds the light within himself, since his spiritual eye was cleansed and fortified by the divine light."[41]

Some of these same meanings associated with the symbol of light have appeared in the Quaker tradition in the thought of George Fox.[42] He describes Light as working to discover and expose sin, to turn people to see the Light, which is Christ, to bring people into an experience of power over sin, to cut out and burn up all evil, and to bring people and nations into the unity of the children of God.[43] Repentance is a turning away from darkness toward the Light and a process of learning to love and walk in that Light. It is an experience of being raised up out of death by the Light that is within.[44] His conviction that Christ, who is the Light, is at work in the midst of darkness is voiced in one of his epistles:

> Sing and rejoice ye Children of the Day, and of the Light;
> for the Lord is at work in this thick Night of Darkness . . .[45]

For Fox, the Light was a promise of life and resurrection for all who would walk in it.[46]

The literature of spirituality is filled with language which uses images associated with light symbolism and tells of a new or transformed vision. Julian of Norwich speaks of being enabled to see with an "inner eye" and tells her readers that eventually she came to see "that our faith is our light in the night, which light is God, our endless day."[47] The conviction that this experience of light and new sight is a gift from God is expressed in the following verse taken from a hymn which is sung by Christians from greatly varied backgrounds and experiences:

> Amazing Grace, how sweet the sound
> that saved a wretch like me.
> I once was lost, but now am found
> was blind, but now I see.

c. Water

Water has always been an extremely significant symbol for communicating the meaning of what it is to be a Christian because of its association with baptism and with the Spirit. That the waters of baptism were experienced as the waters of new life is clear from the art depicted on the walls of the catacombs. Along with portrayals of biblical scenes there are many still life representations of living things such as plants, vines, trees, birds, grapes, etc. These symbols were taken from the culture of the day but were given new meanings by the Christians. Daniélou has suggested that the vine is a variant on the plantation image which signified the Church made up of plants, those people who are to be baptized. God is the gardener and the garden is watered by Christ, the living water.[48] The following selection from an inscription carved around the baptismal font at the Lateran in Rome can give us some idea of the meanings associated with the waters of baptism:

> Here a people of godly race are born for heaven;
> the Spirit gives them life in the fertile waters.
> The Church-Mother, in these waves, bears her children
> like virginal fruit she has conceived by the Holy Spirit. . . .
>
> Sinner, plunge into the sacred fountain to wash away your sin.
> The water receives the old man, and in his place makes the new man to rise.
> You wish to become innocent: cleanse yourself in this bath,
> whatever your burden may be, Adam's sin or your own.
>
> There is no difference between those who are reborn: they are one,
> in a single baptism, a single Spirit, a single faith.
> Let no one be afraid of the number or the weight of his sins:
> He who is born of this stream will be made holy.[49]

It is clear from the above that the waters of baptism were understood as the waters of rebirth and the baptismal font as the fountain of life. The Scriptures offer us two ways of interpreting baptism as an experience of coming to new life. One is that the new life comes through a process of being born again from water and the spirit (Jn 3:3–5), and the other speaks of coming to new life by entering into Christ's death and resurrection (Rom 6:4–5). These two interpretations of baptism found expression in the twofold symbolism of the baptismal font and its waters as womb and as tomb. The earliest interpretation was of the font as mother or womb, and it was not until the third century that the word "tomb" was used in connection with the baptismal rites.[50] In an address to those who had been newly baptized, Cyril of Jerusalem, speaking in the fourth century, combined the two symbols when he said:

> In the same moment you were dying and being born, and that saving water was at once your grave and your mother.[51]

In later centuries the imagery of the struggle between good and evil and that of the suffering and death of Christ would become dominant in the art of baptismal fonts and replace this understanding of the waters as the source of new life.

Water and its associated imagery of thirst was used in the spiritual literature to express the role of the Spirit and to describe the relationship between an individual and God. In her account of the revelation or showings she had received from the Lord, Julian of Norwich, writing in the fourteenth century, uses the imagery of thirst, Christ's and her own, to express the desire and mutual longing which was at the heart of her relationship with him.[52] Teresa of Avila, who chose the image of a garden to portray the spiritual life, made use of the symbol of water to describe the four degrees of prayer as the four different ways of watering the garden. The stages, which begin with the drawing of water from a well and progress through the use of a water wheel and the flowing of a river or stream, end with the water being provided by rain, thus showing that as one progresses in prayer, the effort decreases, and the water, the gift of the Spirit, is given by the Lord.[53]

d. Table

In the first few centuries of the Church, the table was a symbol of identification for Christians. Once they had been baptized they were allowed to join the rest of the community at the table, to remember and give thanks for the life and death of Jesus, to share in the bread and drink from the cup. The prayers of praise and thanksgiving proclaimed over the bread and wine and the prayers beseeching the Spirit to come upon these gifts were also prayed for the people who had gathered, that they too might become the body of Christ. The whole life of a Christian was meant to be eucharistic—a life of praise, of sharing, of being transformed by the Spirit.

When the table became an altar, the president of the assembly was a priest, and the language of sacrifice began to eclipse that of a meal, the meanings carried by this symbol within the community also began to change. This development was intensified in the fourth century as the Church reacted to the Arian heresy by using the liturgy to emphasize the divinity of Christ. Ceremonial appropriate for a king was introduced, and in some places the language of fear and awe was used in speaking about the Eucharist.[54] By the eighth and ninth centuries the Eucharist had become "the mystery of God's coming to man, a mystery one must adoringly wonder at and contemplate from afar."[55] At this time an important change took place in the sign of the bread, for the practice of using unleavened bread began, and people no longer brought the bread from their homes.

The change from bread to hosts, the fact that people no longer took an active part in the Eucharist, and the eventual elimination of the chalice from the Communion rite led to a shift in the meanings carried by the symbol of the table within Christian spirituality. With the dominance of sacrificial symbolism, the symbol of the table could no longer function as the center of the identity of the community. The bread, instead of being broken and shared, was now elevated for all to see and adore. The cup, which had once symbolized both the wine of the messianic banquet and the blood of Christ, now referred only to the latter, and was reserved to the priest. The fact that there was no communal participation and minimal sharing in the bread and wine was understandably accompanied by the loss of the significance of the Eucharist as the place to which one would bring gifts for the needy of the community. The Eucharist lost its place at the center of Christian spirituality. Much has been done in the different Christian communities to restore it to this place, and if the meanings which have been masked are reactivated, the bread and the cup may become once again symbols of transformation for Christians, symbols which proclaim that in receiving the bread and drinking from the cup, one assents to the process of ongoing transformation which they symbolize.

e. Cross

The cross has been a central symbol for Christian spirituality from the beginning, and it has carried a variety of meanings for the community. Christians sign themselves with it, use it in their rituals, compose hymns about it, create artistic models of it, and venerate it. The cross is there for all Christians as an interpretation of the meaning of their lives. It is a symbol which evokes anger, dread, awe, sorrow, hope, thanksgiving, and love. It is a symbol which reveals God's love and fidelity as well as human rejection of that love, and it is a symbol which proclaims the cost of following Christ on his journey. It is a revelation of what happens when one allows the Spirit to shape his or her horizon, when one follows the desire to become an authentic person through self-transcendence. As the symbol of total openness to the Spirit it will be in dialectical opposition with the desire to enclose or protect oneself. It will be in the face of the cross that the Christian will become aware of his or her own sinfulness or refusal of the Spirit.

In the art of the early Church the cross never appeared with a corpus on it. When the cross did appear in the art of baptistries it was as a triumphal, life-giving cross, sometimes covered with flowers.[56] The earliest baptismal font shaped in the form of a cross dates from about 316, and research done on cruciform fonts suggests that the cross at this time was a triumphal image and that the cruciform plan of the font commemorates the victory of Christ and therefore accentuates the resurrection aspect of baptism.[57] In the Middle Ages and following, this symbolism would be transformed to that of the suffering and death of Jesus, a factor certainly influenced by the experiences of war and plague undergone by the people of that era.

Anyone who embarks on the journey of following Christ will eventually have to deal with the meaning of the cross, and the literature of spirituality is filled with reflections on its meaning. Perhaps Bonaventure sums up the truth most succinctly. In describing the soul's journey into God he says:

> There is no other path but through the burning love of the Crucified, a love which so transformed Paul into Christ . . . that he could say: With Christ I am nailed to the cross. I live now, not I, but Christ lives in me (Gal 2:20).[58]

The only way of passing over to the Father is with and through the crucified Christ.[59] However, the Christian is one who believes that the passage through death terminates in life, one who can stand in front of the cross and sing: "I know that my Redeemer liveth."

5. CONCLUSION

The meaning of Christian spirituality is to be found in the lives of all those who live within a horizon illumined by the light of Christ, who come to him in prayer and worship to hear the word of life, who are always being reborn in the waters of his Spirit, who gather with others to share the bread and cup of his life and struggle to allow his meaning to become incarnate in their lives, who do all this in the face of the cross because they believe and hope in the possibility of a new creation. The Christian spiritual life is one of ongoing transformation which becomes evident in a new way of living. It is the story of the human spirit responding to the same Holy Spirit who anointed and led Jesus.

The early Christians have given us a criterion for judging the authenticity of the lives of those who share in Jesus' anointing. It is to be found in the words placed by them on the lips of Jesus as an interpretation of his own anointing, and anyone who claims to live by the Spirit of Jesus must listen to his message.

> Then Jesus, armed with the power of the Spirit, returned to Galilee; and reports about him spread through the whole countryside. He taught in their synagogues and all men sang his praises.
>
> So he came to Nazareth, where he had been brought up, and went to the synagogue on the Sabbath day as he regularly did. He stood up to read the lesson and was handed the scroll of the prophet Isaiah. He opened the scroll and found the passage which says,
>
> The spirit of the Lord is upon me
> because he has anointed me;
> he has sent me to announce good news to the poor,
> to proclaim release for prisoners
> and recovery of sight for the blind;
> to let the broken victims go free,
> to proclaim the year of the Lord's favor (Lk 4:14–19).

NOTES

1. For a presentation of Bernard Lonergan's theory of subjectivity, cf. his article, "The Subject," in William Ryan, Bernard Tyrell, eds. *A Second Collection* (Philadelphia: Westminster Press, 1974), pp. 69–86; also Bernard Lonergan, *Method in Theology* (New York: Herder & Herder, 1972), chapters 1–4.

2. Lonergan calls this "sublation" in "The Subject," *art. cit.,* p. 80.

3. For the fifth level, cf. Bernard Lonergan, *Philosophy of God and Theology* (Philadelphia: Westminster Press, 1973), p. 38; also Robert Doran, "Jungian Psychology and Christian Spirituality," in *Review for Religious* 38, No. 4 (July 1979) 508.

4. Robert Doran, "Jungian Psychology and Christian Spirituality," *art. cit.,* 509; also *idem,* "Psyche, Evil, and Grace," in *Communio* VI, No. 2 (Summer 1979) 202.

5. For Bernard Lonergan's notion of "horizon," cf. *Method in Theology, op. cit.,* pp. 235ff.

6. *Ibid.,* pp. 237ff.

7. *Ibid.,* p. 32.

8. *Ibid.,* p. 57.

9. Edward Schillebeeckx, *Jesus: An Experiment in Christology* (New York: Seabury Press, 1979), p. 257.

10. Aidan Kavanagh, *The Shape of Baptism: The Rite of Christian Initiation* (New York: Pueblo, 1978), p. 17.

11. Edward Schillebeeckx, *op. cit.,* pp. 137–138.

12. *Ibid.,* p. 498.

13. *Ibid.,* p. 667.

14. Joachim Jeremias, *The Lord's Prayer* (Philadelphia: Fortress Press, 1964), p. 20.

15. Edward Schillebeeckx, *op. cit.,* pp. 266–267.

16. *Ibid.,* p. 263.

17. *Ibid.,* pp. 140, 143.

18. *Ibid.,* pp. 206–218.

19. *Ibid.,* p. 309.

20. *Ibid.,* p. 310.

21. *Ibid.,* p. 397.

22. Aidan Kavanagh, *op. cit.,* p. 25.

23. Edward Schillebeeckx, *op. cit.,* p. 378.

24. Michael McDermott, "The Biblical Doctrine of KOINONIA," in *Biblische Zeitschrift* 19 (1975) 67, 70.

25. *Ibid.,* pp. 70–71.

26. Michael A. Fahey, "Ecclesial Community as Communion," in *The Jurist* 36 (1976) 13.

27. Michael McDermott, *op. cit.,* p. 72.

28. *Ibid.,* p. 75.

29. Bernard Cooke, *Ministry to Word and Sacraments* (Philadelphia: Fortress Press, 1976), p. 246; cf. chapters 8–13 for a history of ministry to the word.

30. Johann Arndt, *True Christianity* (New York: Paulist Press, 1979), p. 49.

31. Justin Martyr, "The First Apology," in E.C. Whitaker, ed., *Documents of the Baptismal Liturgy* (London: SPCK, 1970), p. 2.

32. Gregory of Nyssa, *The Life of Moses* (New York: Paulist Press, 1978), pp. 80, 82, 95.

33. George Maloney, *The Mystic of Fire and Light: St. Symeon the New Theologian* (Denville: Dimension Books, 1975), pp. 43, 52.

34. *Ibid.,* p. 64.

35. *Ibid.,* pp. 71–72.

36. John of the Cross, "The Dark Night," in Kieran Kavanagh and Otilio Rodriguez, trs., *The Collected Works of St. John of the Cross* (Washington, D.C.: ICS Publications, 1973), p. 295.

37. *Ibid.,* p. 318.

38. *Ibid.,* pp. 335, 360.

39. *Ibid.,* p. 350.

40. John of the Cross, "The Living Flame of Love," in *op. cit.,* pp. 578–580.

41. *Ibid.,* pp. 587–588.

42. T. Canby Jones, "The Nature and Functions of the Light in the Thought of George Fox," in *Quaker Religious Thought* 16, Nos. 1–2 (Winter 1974–75) 53–71.

43. *Ibid.,* p. 53.

44. *Ibid.,* pp. 58–59.

45. *Ibid.,* p. 67.

46. *Ibid.*

47. Julian of Norwich, *Showings* (New York: Paulist Press, 1978), pp. 312, 322.

48. Jean Daniélou, *Primitive Christian Symbols* (London: Burns & Oates, 1964), pp. 26–38.

49. Lucien Deiss, ed., *Early Sources of the Liturgy* (Collegeville: Liturgical Press, 1967), p. 197.

50. Walter M. Bedard, *The Symbolism of the Baptismal Font in Early Christian Thought* (Washington, D.C.: Catholic University, 1951), pp. 42–43.

51. Cyril of Jerusalem, "Second Lecture on the Mysteries" #4, in *The Fathers of the Church* (Washington, D.C.: Catholic University, 1970), Vol. 64, p. 165.

52. Julian of Norwich, *op. cit.,* pp. 230, 231, 304, 326.

53. Teresa of Avila, "The Book of Her Life," Chapter 11, #7, in Kieran Kavanagh and Otilio Rodriguez, trs., *The Collected Works of St. Teresa of Avila* (Washington, D.C.: ICS Publications, 1976) I, p. 81.

54. John Chrysostom, "Homily 24 on 1 Corinthians," in André Hamman,

ed., *The Mass: Ancient Liturgies and Patristic Texts* (New York: Alba House, 1967), p. 164.

55. Joseph Jungmann, *The Mass of the Roman Rite* (New York: Benziger, 1950) I, p. 84.

56. J.G. Davies, *The Architectural Setting of Baptism* (London: Barrie & Rockliff, 1962), pp. 35–36.

57. Walter M. Bedard, *op. cit.,* pp. 37–40.

58. St. Bonaventure, *The Soul's Journey Into God* (New York: Paulist Press, 1978), p. 54.

59. *Ibid.,* p. 116.

3.
Daily Prayer in Christian Tradition and Life

Gabe Huck

I. THE MEANING OF RITUAL

A 1978 statement of the United States Catholic Bishops' Committee on the Liturgy gave strong expression to an important bit of common sense:

> Each Church gathers regularly to praise and thank God, to remember and make present God's great deeds, to offer common prayer, to realize and celebrate the Kingdom of peace and justice. That action of the Christian assembly is liturgy.[1]

Liturgy is the deed of the assembly, the regular deed. It is, as the word intends, the work of and for the people. Being regular, being the deed of many, liturgy is more the expression of attitude than of emotion; it is about what we mean, not how we feel.[2] It is ritual: word, sound, gesture and the patterns of these.

This realization of our liturgy, the common ritual prayer, as the work of the assembly has been gradually clarified through the liturgical renewal and especially since the *Constitution on the Sacred Liturgy* of Vatican II. The reform of Roman Catholic liturgical books could not put a new vision of liturgy into practice; it could only supply the means for a long-range task. The reformed Rituals insist again and again that it is the assembly that prays, and that the various ministries emerge with the gifts and roles that serve the assembly.[3] The long-range task is far more difficult: whence the ability to do ritual? How to do that giving of thanks and praise each Sunday, that initiating through the year and toward the Easter Triduum, that anointing of the sick and burying of the dead? How to gather, to move, to sing, to be silent, to speak and to listen, to be around a font or a table? How to do the patterns of word and silence, melody and gesture that do, in fact, give full expression to all that we mean and believe?

The ritual deed can become empty. That we know. Yet it is the only deed which can embrace all that we are. One of the documents mentioned above makes it clear: "God does not need liturgy; people do, and people have only their own arts and styles of expression with which to celebrate."[4] These arts and these styles of expression are our concern here. The liturgy in all its manifestations is not, if it is the deed of the assembly, some aspect of a church that runs one track while the very spirit of that people, this thing called spirituality, runs another. The task, one that may be seen in terms of generations, of liturgical renewal, is in re-establishing the bond between this people's spirit and their prayer.

The specific concern here is with the way ritual prayer is known day-by-day, the way a church has received and handed on the rituals of individuals and of households. In that setting the individual will come to know the way of prayer, will come to know the arts and the styles of expression that can then be exercised in the larger assembly. The many difficulties encountered by individuals and families testify to the importance of this area.

> The more [family prayer] is caught up in the crisis of prayer, subjected to restriction and quite often totally overwhelmed in our modern world, the more clearly we feel that here is the true birth-place of common prayer. A child who has never prayed at home with parents and brothers and sisters is denied an essential element in his or her capacity for worship.[5]

The way this particular people, this church, is to become itself, become able to make the signs for what it means and believes and so continue to struggle and bring those meanings and beliefs into its life, depends on our having the ritual of everyday. It is there in the little passages—from sleeping to waking, from alone to together, from hunger to table, from work to leisure, from waking to sleeping—that we are doers of ritual, making the signs that express and inspire our lives.

What follows, then, is a consideration of these daily rites in some parts of the Christian tradition: the prayer of the morning, of the evening, of the table, of the night. This is not a cataloguing of practices but an attempt to see the spirit that keeps the Church in our daily praying. Out of this, we will turn to some of the characteristics of our ritual prayer.

II. THE RHYTHM OF EVERYDAY

1. The Morning

What is the prayer of the morning for Christians? Very early Christian writings take it for granted that Christians pray in the morning.[6] Different sources allude to kneeling and prostration with this prayer (Tertullian)[7] and prayer with washing of the hands (Hippolytus).[8] On occasion, this prayer meant a gathering of people, but usually it is the prayer of the individual or of the household.

The prayer of the morning is always the prayer of praise. It is called forth now as ever by the rising sun: our world is light again. We are rising up like this sun. Sin and death, which the nighttime seemed to shelter, are defeated. Even the daytime may be filled with the works of darkness, with hardship, hurt, sadness, ingratitude, frustration. But morning's prayer proclaims that praise which knows that God's love will prevail. St. Basil said, "We may take nothing in hand until we have been gladdened by the thought of God . . . or set our bodies to any task before we do what has been said: 'We will pray to you, Lord, and you will hear my voice in the morning.' "[9]

That is echoed by Dietrich Bonhoeffer:

> For Christians the beginning of the day should not be burdened and oppressed with besetting concerns for the day's work. At the threshold of the new day stands the Lord who made it. All the darkness and distraction of the dreams of night retreat before the clear light of Jesus Christ and his wakening Word. All unrest, all impurity, all care and anxiety flee before him.[10]

And it is echoed by the poetry of our morning hymns as in this verse by St. Ambrose:

> The Father sends his Son, our Lord,
> To be his bright and shining Word;

> Come, Lord, rise out your gleaming course
> And be our dawn, our light's true source.[11]

Something of this tradition is caught in a very different way by the poet Anne Sexton who recounts the objects and gestures of rising and then states:

> All this is God,
> right here in my pea-green house
> each morning
> and I mean,
> though often forget,
> to give thanks,
> to faint down by the kitchen table
> in a prayer of rejoicing
> as the holy birds at the kitchen window
> peck into their marriage of seeds.[12]

Against this, we place the human experience of the morning which knows something of pressures or of oppression, of routine, of anxiety, of cold. This praise, running from our origins till now, has not been hampered. Morning's prayer has not been the reaction to the moment, the outpouring of feelings. The ritual prayer of morning rises not from the hour's emotions but from the posture of the whole being before the Lord.

The roots of this Christian praying are clearly in the ancient Jewish benedictions of morning:

> Blessed art thou, O Lord our God, King of the universe, who openest the eyes of the blind.
> Blessed art thou, O Lord our God, King of the universe, who clothest the naked.
> Blessed art thou, O Lord our God, King of the universe, who raisest up them that are bowed down.[12a]

These blessings, these simple praises of creation's God, accompany the gestures of early morning. We open our eyes, we clothe ourselves, we straighten up and begin the tasks of the day, with a murmur of praise, a blessing of the Lord. Here is indeed a consciousness of the troubles of the world, of the morning with its cares. Who is blind? Who bowed down? Who naked? We say: it is myself, this wakened creature, myself insofar as I can stand with the blind, the naked, the oppressed. The simple words of the prayer unite the praise of the Creator with the awareness of evil, of pain and of bitterness permeating the creation. Though these benedictions long ago left the Christian's vocabulary of prayer, their spirit has remained.

That spirit is worded by the Gospel canticle long associated with morning's prayer, the *Benedictus* (Lk 1:67–79). Not only that it begins with the blessing of God ("Blessed be the Lord, the God of Israel"), or that it uses the image of the rising sun for the coming of the Messiah, but it knows a world of enemies and fear and sin from which the Lord whom we praise is delivering us.

The sign of the cross, with which the Christian is first marked in preparation for baptism, has endured as a ritual of the morning when much else has been lost. The way the sign is made may vary, but often without any words at all the beginning of the day is marked with this sign. In origin, the tracing of a cross on the body may not have been related to the cross of Jesus but rather to the unknown name of God,[13] a way of identifying oneself with the group of believers. As a prayer of the morning, it is a wordless naming both of oneself and of the Lord. It is remembering, it is dedication, it is praise.

Common to Jewish and Christian morning prayer is the morning psalmody, the intoning of Psalms 148, 149 and 150. The first calls for all creation to join in praising the Lord, the second urges praise from those he has chosen, and the third names the music of our praise. Through scores of generations, Jews and Christians have had these words by heart to mark their mornings, to give shape to what morning means, to let the eyes see and the ears hear and the touch sense what it is to be awake and to praise God.

2. *The Evening*

In the early Church, the evening prayer was rooted in the lighting of the lamps and the praise of Christ who is our light. The second century hymn *Phos Hilaron* continues to express this:

> O gracious Light,
> pure brightness of the everliving Father in heaven,
> O Jesus Christ, holy and blessed.
>
> Now as we come to the setting of the sun,
> and our eyes behold the vesper light,
> we sing thy praises, O God: Father, Son, and Holy Spirit.

> Thou art worthy at all times to be praised by happy voices,
> O Son of God, O Giver of life,
> and to be glorified through all the worlds.[14]

The moment is set aside because light is giving way to darkness, because the rhythms of the daytime end and a different sort of time begins. The deeds and the loving care of God are remembered not in extraordinary circumstances but in this everydayness, in the coming of darkness and the common need to light lamps. God is praised for the light. Here is clearly seen something basic to the ritual prayer of Christians: it does not call for or depend on the unusual, but the ordinary is an epiphany yet remains ordinary. It is a matter of darkness and light, gift of a spinning earth. The sun's passage has compelled notice, to which the ritual adds not so much a viewpoint as a reverence, a way of lighting lamps, a wording of that gesture, the happy thanksgiving.

> No authority can take credit for discovering the significance of morning and evening. Across cultures and peoples, primitive and modern, the start and end of a day have been special, even sacred, times. Here people have acknowledged their relation to the forming and sustaining God and his universe. The sun's journey moves the human spirit like a vast tide, ebb and flow. Whether the words like vespers and evening prayer are used or not, it remains true: a people gathers in prayer, not in response to the *idea* of a sunset, but the *event,* to day's end and night's coming.[15]

The sense for the event supports and is built up by the ritual prayer with which the individual or the household marks the coming of evening. This rite may be as simple as the recitation of the Our Father or the Angelus, or it may mean the worded gesture of lighting a candle in the half-darkness. Done through seasons and years, this response to the presence of God in the meeting of darkness and light assumes and fosters a way of being, a way that may find a variety of expressions or styles in everyday life. Yet, there are limits to that variety and a strong sense, common to all, of God, of humanity, of creation that would bind those who pause for such prayer.

A second element of evening prayer, though one associated also with the night prayer that comes just before retiring, has to do with the burden of the day that has passed. The strongest expression of this is found in the gesture of burning incense, a gesture which has been worded in the liturgy by verses of Psalm 141:

> I have called to you, Lord; hasten to help me!
> Hear my voice when I cry to you.
> Let my prayer arise before you like incense,
> the raising of my hands like an evening oblation.

The words have many associations with the Temple worship and have been related to the gesture of Jesus on the cross, but the action itself primarily counts. What does it mean to put grains of fragrant spices and gums on burning coals and to fill the room with their smoke and sweet smell? At other times incense is burned to honor persons or objects, but here it has to do with a sense for the evils and troubles of the day that are consumed in the burning love of God, the always amazing grace that is so incredibly sweet as it enfolds me.

This element of evening or night prayer has often taken a more verbal form: the recitation of prayers of sorrow and some words of assurance of God's mercy. This might be preceded by a time of silent reflection, examination of conscience when individuals recall the day that is ending and any wrong they have done. Though such a prayer is obviously more compatible with persons who find it difficult to gather for prayer with others, some of the rich ambiguity of the incense-burning is lost, as is the sense for being a Church that remembers and confesses and stands in God's mercy. Yet there is present in the individual kneeling at bedside, striking the breast and repeating an act of contrition, and in the small community standing around the smoking incense, singing the words of Psalm 141, the same sense of what it means to end a day and face the night. In both, the evil of the day is real; it means failure, destruction of what the morning promised, often boredom with a seemingly endless day. It means individual deeds and omissions, the whole struggling way of things. All of this is caught up in the gesture and word of ritual, evening after evening. And with it, not even as a separate word or gesture but as the larger reality that embraces all of this, there is the mystery of the cross, the passover mystery: the ever-present waters of baptism immerse us in this struggle whose outcome we have believed.

Evening's prayer knows a third moment also, one often joined to the night prayer of individuals and families. This is the prayer of intercession. In particular, it is a certain ritual of intercessory prayer, a litany-like series of short prayers that name the general and some particular concerns. Though not peculiar to the evening, this way of praying finds a home here in both the formal and informal prayers of Christians. Bonhoeffer writes well of this:

> This is the appropriate place for common intercessions. After the day's work we pray God for the blessing, peace, and safety of all Christendom: for our congregation; for the pastor and his ministry; for the poor, the wretched, the lonely; for the sick and dying; for our neighbors, for our own folks at home, and for our fellowship. When can we have any deeper sense of God's power and working than in the hour when our hands lay down their work and we commit ourselves to the hands of God? When are we more ready for the prayer of blessing, peace, and preservation than at the time when our own activity ceases? When we grow weary, God does his work.[16]

And of the importance of this way of praying in Christian tradition, Evelyn Underhill writes:

> From every point of view it is plain that the Church's unceasing supplication to God and remembrance before him of all her members—her "great intercession" for their needs and the needs of the world—must form an essential part of her liturgical life. . . . For the Intercession of the Liturgy, though no detailed petition or individual need is too homely to be brought within its radius, is always a corporate action, a reminder of the fact that the Communion of Saints and Communion of Sinners is one Body.[17]

The intercessory prayers of the Church encompass the great litanies of ancient liturgies:

> Let us pray for peace, which is heaven's gift. May the Lord in his mercy give us peace.
> Let us pray for faith. May the Lord give us grace to keep our faith in him untainted to the end.
> Let us pray for the bishop. May our Lord grant him a long life and keep him true to the faith, that breaking the bread of truth as he ought, he may preside over the Church blamelessly and without reproach.
> Let us pray for the whole world. May the Lord provide for all creatures and give to each what is best for it.[18]

We also say the simple prayers learned at bedside by the child: "God, bless Grandma and Grandpa and Uncle Bill. . . ." In all of them there is this gathering up that is the work of the Church, which stands always as interceding for the world. Such prayer is learned in the evening prayer and used at all the great liturgies of the Church. Their strength is not found in turning attention to each individual concern, but in their sweep, in the ritual's rhythm. This is both the recurring rhythm which brings the same petitions back each evening, and the internal rhythm in which the prayers for peace and for individuals and classes of people go on one after another, joined perhaps by a special concern of the day, patterns repeated by heart not so that the mind may be elsewhere but precisely that heart and lips and body may also be praying. In this evening prayer, the Christian becomes petitioner for the world, constant maker of intercessions. Here is learned the relation between the formal and the spontaneous in prayer; here, too, is learned a discipline of prayer whereby the intense desires and needs, which without this discipline may become the only occasion for intercession, are made always in a context shaped by the praying Church.

Other ways of praying have been common to the evening, especially psalmody and the reading of Scripture, but these three moments—a change of rhythm from day to night; examination of conscience in awareness of evil and sin; and intercessory prayers in reliance on God's mercy—seem to constitute what is unique to this hour of prayer. The Lord's Prayer would, as in the morning, be a nearly constant part of the evening prayer, alone or in community.

3. The Night

"At midnight, rise and wash your hands in water and pray."[19] This prayer of night was, at least at some times and places, the practice of the early Church. Though prayer in the middle of sleeping hours did not endure as a common practice, praying at night time, before sleep, has remained a steady part of the prayer ritual of the home. We have already discussed how consciousness of sin and mercy enters into this prayer together with prayers of intercession, but the night prayer is more than this.

As with morning and evening, the prayer is born of the event: the passing from time awake to sleep, from awareness and activity to loss of control. It is the bed and its room that is the space of this prayer. Here is the place of birth, of fear of the dark, of comforting, of rest, of dreams, of lovemaking, of pain, of healing, of anxiety, of weakness, of a final anger and peacemaking, of death.

The texts of night's prayer, from the poetic to the trite, invoke God's protection in the darkness. This fragment is a prayer from the third century:

> Be off, Satan, from this door and from these four walls. This is no place for you; there is nothing for you to do here. This is the place for Peter and Paul and the holy gospel; and this is where I mean to sleep, now that my worship is done, in the name of the Father and of the Holy Spirit.[20]

And this comes from an early English prayer:

> Matthew, Mark, Luke and John,
> Bless the bed that I lie on.
> Before I lay me down to sleep
> I give my soul to Christ to keep.
> Four corners to my bed,
> Four angels there a-spread,
> Two to foot and two to head,
> And four to carry me when I'm dead.
> If any danger come to me,
> Sweet Jesus Christ, deliver me.
> He's the branch and I'm the flower,
> Pray God send me a happy hour,
> And if I die before I wake
> I pray that Christ my soul will take.[21]

It contains much of what has been until now a common night prayer taught to children:

> Now I lay me down to sleep,
> I pray the Lord my soul to keep.
> If I should die before I wake,
> I pray the Lord my soul to take.

The night prayer—Compline, from the Liturgy of the Hours—has long included this blessing:

> May the almighty and merciful Lord give us a peaceful night and a perfect death.

The following hymn is also included:

> As twilight now draws near its close,
> Creator of the world, we pray
> That in your goodness you will be
> Our stronghold till the coming day.
>
> Grant rest without disturbing dreams.
> Let nothing lead us into sin.
> Ward off the evil one's assaults.
> Bless, guard this night we now begin.[22]

This prayer is also part of Compline:

> Visit this dwelling, we ask you, O Lord. Drive far away all the snares of the enemy. Let your holy angels dwell herein and keep us in peace, and let your blessing be always upon us.

The following prayer is taken from a section of family prayers in *The Book of Common Prayer:*

> Defend us from all dangers and mischiefs, and from the fear of them; that we may enjoy such refreshing sleep as may fit us for the duties of the following day. Make us ever mindful of the time when we shall lie down in the dust; and grant us grace always to live in such a state that we may never be afraid to die; so that, living or dying, we may be thine. . . .

Many of the Offices of Compline have included these psalm verses:

> Keep us, O Lord, as the apple of your eye.
> Shelter us in the shadow of your wings.

In the sixth century, when St. Benedict wrote his Rule for monasteries, the psalms of the prayer before retiring were already established: "At Compline, the same psalms are to be repeated every day, namely Psalms 4, 90 and 133."[23]

These psalms were also an ancient part of the evening or night prayer of the Synagogue,[24] but the common images of night prayer shared by

Church and Synagogue go beyond this. The following prayers from the *Siddur* contain many images similar to those in the prayers above:

> Blessed art thou, Lord our God, King of the universe, who closest my eyes in sleep, my eyelids in slumber. May it be thy will, Lord my God and God of my fathers, to grant that I lie down in peace and that I rise up in peace. Let not my thoughts upset me—nor evil dreams, nor sinful fancies. May my family ever be perfect in thy sight. Grant me light, lest I sleep the sleep of death; for it is thou who givest light to the eyes.
>
> Grant, Lord our God, that we lie down in peace, and that we rise again, O our King, to life. Spread over us thy shelter of peace, and direct us with good counsel of thy own. Save us for thy name's sake; shield us, and remove from us the enemy and pestilence, the sword and famine and grief; remove the adversary from before us and from behind us; shelter us in the shadow of thy wings; for thou art our guarding and saving God, indeed, a gracious and merciful God and King.[25]

Night prayer is praying in the dark. It is without books. It is always the same. Because of the event that night is, and still is despite artificial light, despite pace and schedules, it remains a time of ritual prayer. As these prayers of various ages were born of the night event, so they continue to be prayed and to evolve only minimally. For we still know fear at night, and weariness; sleep can still be relished or dreaded. In night and sleep we still recognize a presence of death, not terrible necessarily, but making us uneasy, preparing us. The prayers of the night are a preparing to die, a learning to die, to commend ourselves to the Lord over and over again until we are ready to do so a last time.

In much of Christian tradition, both in the official texts of the Office of Compline and in popular piety, night prayer knows one other element. This is the final song or prayer invoking the protection of the Mother of Jesus. The most familiar form is the *Salve Regina:*

> Mary, we greet thee,
> mother and queen all merciful;
> our life, our sweetness and our hope, we hail thee.
> To thee we exiles, children of Eve, lift our crying.
> To thee we send our sighs, as, mourning and weeping,
> we pass through this vale of sorrow.
> Haste then, we pray, O our intercessor,
> look with pity, with eyes of love compassionate, upon us sinners.

> And after, when this earthly exile shall be ended,
> show us thy womb's most blessed fruit, thy Jesus.
> O clement, O loving, O most sweet virgin Mary.[26]

This is an eleventh century hymn whose continued popularity in Latin hinges not only on the beautiful chant melody but on the association of various fears and prayers of the night with a parent's presence and care. In Catholic piety that presence was at times far closer in the image of the mother, of Mary, than in any accessible image of God.

4. The Prayer at Meals

Here it is not so much a matter of gathering texts, for there are not so many, as of understanding the place of prayer before sharing food. The event is as always to be sought as source of the ritualizing. The crisis today, which extends far beyond the absence or abuse of ritual, is a lack of event. Praying is bound up with the occasion. It suggests some qualities or attitudes toward gathering to share food. Christians are contradicting themselves if on Sundays at the Eucharist they seem to believe in the fellowship of a table, the awesome beauty of bread and wine, the good of human festivity, and yet let daily habit make of the meal something cheap, uncared for, unprotected from frenzy on the one hand and loneliness on the other.

The need for food and the possibility of delight in it, however simple, and in the fellowship of a table are never far from us. That is why we can know the eucharistic table gathering for the ordinary and deeply human event that it is. We are able to find holiness in the bread that is blessed and broken, the cup that is blessed and shared in our assembly; yet that will happen only if we recognize holiness in all the fruit of the earth and work of human hands, by which we are nourished and brought together, day-in and day-out. The language of the Christian Eucharist is the language of the kitchen, the dining room, the soup line, and more:

> However elegant the knowledge of the diningroom may be, it begins in the soil, in the barnyard, in the slaughterhouse; amid the quiet violence of the garden, strangled cries, and fat spitting in the pan. Table manners depend on something's having been grabbed by the throat.[27]

The holiness of the Eucharist happens for us because we know first and well the holiness of every table where food and self are shared.

Practical problems cannot be separated from the matter of table prayer. The failure of individuals and households to ritualize this moment with more than one or two formulas, or with constant use of spontaneous prayer, witnesses not only our lack of sense of doing the Eucharist as table prayer, but also the lack of importance placed in food itself and in the sharing of the table. Providing patterns of prayer is not enough. We have to deal with the difficulties of regularly shared meals in the household, with our need to have reverence for food and respect for its preparation, with ways of gathering and waiting upon one another, with lingering and sharing the day's story, with learning about biblical justice, reminding us that we do not sit down to table alone but the whole hungry world sits here with us.

Balthasar Fischer has written of the close connection between the Eucharist and the table prayers of the home in the Church's early centuries. He notes that eucharistic formulae occur in monastic table prayers but believes them closely related to family customs.[28] He further notes of the ritual of the table:

> Together with such formulae of blessing for the table, there must have been also at an early stage the singing of Psalms and hymns at family meals, even if only, perhaps, on special occasions. . . . The custom of surrounding meal-times with religious song, which can be explained in terms both of the heritage of Judaism and of opposition to comparable pagan customs, is at all events in essence older than the fourth century. It is attested for Alexandria by Clement, for North Africa by Cyprian. Even in Tertullian's time it is a matter of course that Christians will pray and make the sign of the cross before eating.[29]

We are peoples of the table, which is, according to Edmond Barbotin, "the social furnishing."

> It is, to begin with, the piece of furniture made for reunions; being accessible from all sides, the table is made to be surrounded. . . . It is here that the family, daily scattered, is daily reunited.[30]

At table, every meal is to be a communion: in its sharing of food, in the way we partake of that food, in our conversation. When the sense of this ordinary communion at table is felt, the blessing, called so well the "grace," is at home. It is in the ritual of gathering, in song or word or gesture or even silence that the meaning of this communion comes alive.

III. SOME MARKS OF RITUAL PRAYER

Ritual prayer throughout the rhythms of the day, week, seasons and even the passages of life does its work. Here, out of the above reflections, are a number of important facets of the presence of such ritual in the Church.

1. We Recognize One Another

Ritual prayer means a sense of being a people. We are not first of all to recognize ourselves and one another because of membership in ecclesial institutions, or because we share something resembling common moral convictions, or because we can agree about the nature of evil and grace. We sense first that we belong to one another because we sing the same songs to the Lord. There is a universe of local expression in prayer, binding together the Church in a region, a parish even. There also is a universe of common expression, rooted in the words and gestures of our Scriptures, that make a home of the Church not only across cultures but across time. It is a home in which Jew and Christian share much.

We recognize one another in the breaking of the bread, in constant thanksgiving, in a thrice said "Holy," in the cross traced on our bodies, in calling God "Our Father." In such expressions are contained all the rest, dogma and morality and institutional necessities.

The quality of appropriateness, suggested in *Environment and Art in Catholic Worship,* might be broadly applied here to the arts which make up any ritual prayer:

> It must be capable of bearing the weight of mystery, awe, reverence, and wonder which the liturgical action expresses.[31]

Ritual prayer must so bear the weight. It must be strong enough, beautiful enough, poetic enough, and simply tough enough to bear the weight of mystery in its repetition, of reverence as it is passed from generation to generation. At every level, from the household to the largest understandings of Church, we need some words and sounds and gestures of prayer that bear the weight of being the Church, that build a sense of belonging, that let us know we are at home here.

2. The Troubles of the World

Our ritual prayer binds us to the world that is, not only in intercession for the daily bread and a reign of God in a foreign land, but even more in the prayer known by heart, the sounds and looks and tastes of what humans have made of life always. We can consider only the prayer of one season, Advent, in this context.

The prayer of Advent, even if limited to a few burning candles, a circle of green stuff grown from the earth, silence, and verses of the "O" antiphons in "O come, O come, Emmanuel," still has its particular sound, look, poetry. Somehow, these can make us dwell behind bars in Attica Prison, behind bolted doors in lonely apartment houses, behind facades of all kinds in faces, parties and nations. Advent's sound, look, pace—these speak of what it is to be afraid and know what it is to hear a promise. Fear and promise are in our very soul. It makes no difference that we have uttered this prayer before, that we know it through and through. Or rather, it does make a difference, for, as we know this way of praying more and more by heart, it is set free within us. Its origins are in the human heart. It is never something clever, something nice. Set free, the light and darkness and all the images they call up within can gather and hold the tensions and contradictions of the world in those mighty names we name: O Dawn, O Key of David, O Lord. Advent's prayer speaks to and for the bully in us as well as the coward, the prophet as well as the plodder, the clown as well as the bystander. With all those ears we listen, with all those eyes we look, with all those tongues we come to make an Advent prayer.

The ritual keeps the Church all bound up in the troubles of the world and its gladness, too. Never can we pray our songs and psalms with our backs to suffering. When we pray as the people of the Bible, and as the people baptized, then that book and those waters set us down deeply in creation's struggle, in the evil we continue to do to one another.

3. The Ritual Prayer Is Ordinary

Ritual prayers are there to be murmured day and night by ordinary people. It is the Angelus, for instance, that prayer of noon, whatever be the feelings of the day, the grasping for a moment of what Incarnation means to this earth. Ritual prayer, familiar prayer, opens our eyes and ears to the ordinary, creates deep thankfulness that our home is within the ordinary. The ritual prayer comes when it comes, at its set hour, day, season. It comes, however we feel. It does not change anything but our perspective.

Prayer by heart that marks the hours or the seasons, slowly becoming almost physical, part of breathing, has this possibility toward the everydayness, the ordinary: even while it reveals the wonders there, it opens eyes and ears and noses and mouths, it makes this space and time of ours wonderful, precisely as ordinary, as the abode of God within us. Like the tea ceremony as Okakura reveals it, the repeated prayers of everyday are about "the utmost beatitude of the mundane."[32]

4. Playfulness

There is a distancing and playfulness, a sense of humor in the ritual prayers that carry us along. Again, it puts us, and all else, in perspective. That is said of the tea ceremony:

> For Teaism is the art of concealing beauty that you may discover it, of suggesting what you dare not reveal. It is the noble secret of laughing at yourself, calmly yet thoroughly, and is thus humor itself.[33]

In prayer we are playing with perspective, divining things in our borderline mystical way. What else can it be but a refusal to buy the world's absolutes that lets us banish the "alleluia" from our prayers for a certain forty days and stuff it into every cranny of prayer for the next fifty? How could that be important?

We have been told that ritual shares much with play, especially in its impracticality, its carelessness of time, its calling into question idols known as "priorities." The ritual prayer does this daily, weekly, and through our great seasons. The terrible, one-dimensional life that presses down on us in our culture is shattered by prayer which opens us to other dimensions. The old woman making the Stations of the Cross, the Moslem bowing deeply toward Mecca, the Jew murmuring a blessing over a piece of bread: such rhythms in one's life tumble many of the world's absolutes. They will not stand, are undermined, doomed.

In *The Coup,* John Updike tells how the disguised ruler of a poverty-ridden African land came quite by accident to find a new city near the northern border of his country. He wanders about observing how foreign money has discovered oil and established overnight a whole new way of life. He sees the people, some only recently come from tribal life, going about their new jobs, living in their new homes, buying at their new stores.

> The business of oil, the businesses that cluttered around the business of oil, pre-empted the mental spaces formerly devoted to battle and ritual, death and God, so that these last two came to loom as not only strangers

> but monsters, unthinkables, like the abstract formulae of science whereby oil was lifted from its porous matrix and its tangled molecules sorted into saleable essences. The volume of mysteries upon which men float had been displaced.[34]

The prayer of everyday can resist this take-over of consciousness. It keeps us aware that death and God are fellow players in our world, demands that we put self and world in that perspective. Accustomed to play daily with notions of God, death, saints, evil and grace, we know a many-dimensioned world. Steady prayer means keeping that "volume of mysteries."

5. Praying from Need

A person must need to pray, not ought to pray, or want to pray. The story told in the film *Lies My Father Told Me* illustrates this. We watch a three-generation Jewish family in a Canadian city at the turn of the century. The grandfather is a man whose life is filled with prayer, from the morning benedictions as he rises and washes, to his mumbled words and gestures of prayer throughout the day; he travels the alleys with his horse and wagon looking for junk to buy and sell. His son-in-law also keeps the faith, but has no time or need for such piety. His life is about work, about getting the family out of their tenement apartment and their poverty. This man worries about his young son because of the boy's love and devotion for the grandfather. The fear he has for his son is not that the boy will be religious, a believer, for that would be acceptable. He fears that the boy will somehow follow the grandfather's ways and fashion a life that could not be lived without prayer, a life that truly needs prayer.

Such a life makes religion more than an institution, a fellowship, shared principles and history. Our age knows much of creating needs, but the need to pray has been conquered like a disease. We do not acquire the habit of regularly sharing in the words and chants and gestures that would question and even break so many other needs. Yet, it is only from need that the ritual prayer can come, from facing God's presence and what that does to all other presences, from groping for some ways to acknowledge, respond and keep in touch with Him.

CONCLUSION

The tradition we have received evolves rituals. Using time, place, things of nature and of human creation, word, sound, movement and all the senses—either one of these or many, ordered by formalized art or folk art, established through repetition—rituals transcend the limited dimensions of everyday and so express and inspire a way of living. At their best, they are rich and ambiguous enough to do this. Rituals interpret for us the passages of our lives, through the periodic practices of initiation, through the marking of anniversaries of persons and events, through the week's beginning on the Lord's Day and gathering for the Eucharist, through the individual or household rites that mark each day. A person's spirit, a local community's spirit, and the spirit of an entire Church is most complete and fulfilled in the moments of ritual. In ritual's storytelling, in its music and dance, in its silence and hospitality, the Church is kept true to itself and its Lord, recognizes itself, and names the false gods to be such. A person living by that spirit, the day-in and day-out living that is the very soul of the Church, will need the everyday rituals of mornings and nights. In these we do name ourselves and find what we mean.

NOTES

1. *Environment and Art in Catholic Worship* (Washington, D.C.: United States Catholic Conference, 1978), n. 9.

2. Cf. Susanne Langer, *Philosophy in a New Key* (New York: Mentor Books), p. 134: "A rite regularly performed is the constant reiteration of sentiments toward 'first and last things'; it is not a free expression of emotions, but a disciplined rehearsal of 'right attitudes'." Also helpful is Abraham Heschel's insight: "Emotion is an important component of prayer, but the primary presupposition is conviction. If such conviction is lacking, if the presence of God is a myth, then prayer to God is a delusion. . . . The source of prayer then is an insight rather than an emotion. It is the insight into the mystery of reality; it is, first of all, the sense of the ineffable that enables us to pray. As long as we refuse to take notice of what is beyond our sight, beyond our reason, as long as we are blind to the mystery of being, the way to prayer is closed to us. If the rising of the sun is but a daily routine of nature there is no reason for us to praise the Lord for the sun and for the life we live": "Prayer as Discipline," in *The Insecurity of Freedom* (New York: Farrar, Straus & Giroux, 1967), pp. 258–259.

3. Cf., e.g., *Rite of Christian Initiation of Adults* (Washington, D.C.: United States Catholic Conference, 1974), n. 41; *Rite of Baptism for Children* (Washington, D.C.: United States Catholic Conference, 1970), n. 4. The point is best made in *Environment and Art in Catholic Worship, op. cit.,* nn. 9, 28, 29, 63.

4. *Environment and Art in Catholic Worship, op.cit.,* n. 4.

5. Balthasar Fischer, "The Common Prayer of Congregation and Family in the Ancient Church," in *Studia Liturgica* 10 (1974) 117.

6. "As soon as they wake in the morning, before they do anything else, let all the faithful, men and women, wash their hands and pray to God, and then let them go about their business." From "Apostolic Tradition," in Jacques Zeiller, ed., *Christian Beginnings* (New York: Hawthorn Books, 1960), p. 122.

7. Cf. the summary of Tertullian's treatise "On Prayer" in *National Bulletin on Liturgy* 58, pp. 81–82.

8. From "Apostolic Tradition," *art. cit.*

9. *Ibid.*

10. Dietrich Bonhoeffer, *Life Together* (New York: Harper & Row, 1954), p. 43.

11. From "O splendor of the Father's light" by St. Ambrose; cf. any monastic *Book of Hours.*

12. Anne Sexton, *The Awful Rowing toward God* (Boston: Houghton Mifflin, 1975), "Welcome Morning," p. 58.

12a. Cf. *Authorized Daily Prayer Book* (New York: Hebrew Publishing, n.d.), p.6.

13. Cf. Marion Hatchett, *Sanctifying Life, Time and Space* (New York: Seabury Press, 1976), pp. 17, 37. Cf. also Jean Daniélou, *Primitive Christian Symbols* (Baltimore: Helicon, 1963), chapter on "The Taw Sign." Also, from "Apostolic Tradition," *art. cit.*: "Do your best at all times to make the sign of the cross on your forehead worthily. The sign of the passion. . . ." This quotation from Hippolytus indicates that by the third century the association with Jesus' crucifixion was recognized. Interestingly, the words that eventually became associated with the gesture refer again to the name of God, "In the name of the Father and of the Son and of the Holy Spirit."

14. Translation from *The Book of Common Prayer* (New York: Church Hymnal Corp., 1976).

15. Laurence Mayer, "The Shape of Our Evening Prayer," in *Evening Prayer in the Parish* (Chicago: Liturgy Training Publications, 1981), p. 2.

16. Dietrich Bonhoeffer, *op. cit.,* pp. 73–74.

17. Evelyn Underhill, *Worship* (New York: Harper, 1936), pp. 150–151.

18. André Hamman, *Early Christian Prayers* (Chicago: Henry Regnery, 1961), p. 138.

19. From "Apostolic Tradition," *art. cit.,* p. 123.

20. André Hamman, *op. cit.,* p. 238.

21. *Ibid.*

22. Translation of "Te lucis ante terminum," in William Storey, *Lord, Hear Our Prayer* (Notre Dame: Ave Maria Press, 1978), p. 27.

23. *St. Benedict's Rule for Monasteries* (Collegeville: Liturgical Press, 1948), Chapter 18, p. 39. In the Hebrew enumeration, these are Psalms 4, 91, 134.

24. Eric Werner, *The Sacred Bridge* (New York: Schocken, 1970), p. 145.

25. *Daily Prayer Book* (New York: Hebrew Publishing, 1949), pp. 780, 782.

26. Cf. any monastic *Book of Hours.*

27. Aidan Kavanagh, *The Shape of Baptism* (New York: Pueblo, 1978), p. 160.

28. Balthasar Fischer, *art. cit.,* p. 119. Cf. also, Robert Ledogar, "Table Prayers and Eucharist," in Herman Schmidt, ed., *Prayer and Community* (New York: Herder & Herder, 1970).

29. Balthasar Fischer, *art. cit.,* p. 119.

30. Edmond Barbotin, *The Humanity of Man* (Maryknoll: Orbis, 1975), p. 320.

31. *Environment and Art in Catholic Worship, op. cit.,* n. 21.

32. Okakura Kakuzo, *The Book of Tea* (Tokyo: Charles Tuttle, 1956), p. 33.

33. *Ibid.,* p. 15.

34. John Updike, *The Coup* (New York: Knopf, 1978), p. 263.

4.
God the Lawgiver—Meditations on the Spirituality of the Halakha

Norman Solomon

" 'The Lord is a man of war; the Lord is His name!' (Ex 15:3) . . . at the (Red) Sea He appeared (to Israel) as a warrior engaged in battle . . . at Sinai He revealed Himself as an old man steeped in compassion. . . ."

So runs an early Midrash,[1] concerned above all to demonstrate that, notwithstanding His protean multiplicity of appearance, God is One and His name is One.

Now to Rome! Present yourself at San Pietro in Vincoli, and behold there Michelangelo's powerful sculpture of Moses—Moses the Lawgiver, as Philo called him.[2] This Moses is no benign sage, but a stern warrior, his countenance etched with determination and authority, demanding obedience to the heavenly ideals inscribed upon the Tables of the Law he so firmly grasps.

Yet *God* the Lawgiver appears "as an old man steeped in mercy. . . ." And of Moses Scripture avers: "The man, Moses, was more humble than any upon the earth" (Num 12:3).

Philo, my brother of Alexandria, first of those who[3] spoke the words of Japhet in the tents of Shem, for a thousand wise words I praise you, but for two foolish ones I sigh—that you confuse God the Lawgiver with His spokesman Moses, and that Torah for you is *nomos,* the Law, not *hodos,* the Way.

Michelangelo Buonarroti, my Florentine cousin, whose incised forms so marvelously mimic the handwork of your Creator, it is not Moses our teacher you have wrought in stone, but some magnificent Renaissance prince, a "universal man" to rule in glory rather than a patient shepherd of the flock of Israel.

I. SPIRITUALITY OF THE SOURCE

The spirituality of Torah is the spirituality of its Source. Rules and counsel, observations about the world, wise sayings, may be described as "spiritual" when, if heeded, they tend to result in actions characteristic of the spiritual life, and indeed this is often enough the way of the words of Torah; the rule that one should pray to God three times a day tends, if heeded, to produce spiritual awareness, independently of the source from which the rule emanates. But this is not the *characteristic* spirituality of Torah; the special spirituality possessed by *all* words of Torah, irrespective of whether or not, if they were detached from the Torah-matrix, they would tend to produce spirituality in those who heeded them, is the spirituality of their Source. They are Words of God. This is just as true of, say, the talmudic regulations about price-fixing or circumstantial evidence or mixed seeds or the dietary laws as it is of the commandments to love one's neighbor or to imitate the ways of God. Herein lies the beauty of *halakha.* It tells us that *all life matters*, that whatever we do has significance, that there are not two worlds, one for Caesar and one for God, but that *sacredness* must reach all thoughts and deeds. Thus the rabbis[4] denounce as a heretic one who denies that "the Torah is from heaven,"[5] one who claims that even some little part of it was composed by Moses "out of his own mind." To conceive of a human being, even Moses, as "the Lawgiver" is to deny the transcendent Source of Torah, thus to undermine its unity and spirituality; for the moment that Moses, and not God, is its author, Torah is fragmented, and each statement in it can stand only on its intrinsic merits, its spirituality deriving from its specific content rather than from its Source. "The Holy One, Blessed be He, and the Torah are one."[6]

What is the position of the thinker today who cannot, on scholarly and historical grounds, accept the medieval view of Torah as the Word of God accurately recorded by Moses and faithfully interpreted by the rabbis in accordance with principles deriving directly from God and handed down through Moses by word of mouth? The question becomes even more acute if, as I shall shortly argue, there is a substantial human involvement in Torah, even as conceived by the rabbis of the Talmud.

Undoubtedly a "fundamentalist" attitude makes it easier to appreciate Torah as the Word of God and thus as the transcendental backing for our principles and rules of human behavior. But we cannot support fundamentalism just on the grounds that it simplifies our theology. If it is wrong it is wrong, and the decision must be made with greater weight attached to objective evidence—which is after all one of God's main channels of communication with us—than to theological convenience.

The non-fundamentalist nevertheless has many ways open to him to handle language in such a way as to legitimize speaking of Torah as the Living Word of God. I shall indicate what I conceive as the *minimum* requirement for this; the closer one's general theological outlook is to full-fledged fundamentalism, the more one may add in terms of historical definiteness, and the more one will reject of modern historical study of our religious source-texts.

What, then, is the minimum content to be given to such a phrase as "God commanded me to . . ." so that it retains useful meaning? We must assess this in terms of its *experiential* content; we must ask, for instance: To what sort of experience does the Book of Leviticus refer when it says: "And the Lord spoke to Moses saying . . ."? The answer will be along the lines that the verse asserts Moses had an overwhelming sense that the words he spoke were (a) rooted in something beyond and entirely different from himself—"transcendent"—something he would in other contexts refer to as Creator, and which possessed a definite moral dimension, and (b) that his words were *significant* with regard to the ultimate concerns of life.

If we approach the contemporary Torah-oriented Jew and ask him to describe his experience in terms of this sort we will come up with something rather more complex, for the contemporary Jew would be describing, not an experience of the form "God told me to . . ." but rather what it means to him to learn, to understand, a statement of Torah which, emanating from God, has been mediated through an age-old tradition traced back to Moses; or what it means to him to perform a commandment, a *mitzvah,* of that Torah. Let us describe his experience of giving alms to the needy. If we say, "He sits at his desk and writes out a check to a charitable organization," we are accurately describing his *action,* but we are indicating nothing of his experience, certainly nothing of its "spirituality" or otherwise. Merely writing out a check need not be a spiritual experience at all; a person might do it out of habit or compulsion, and even if he does it voluntarily it may be a generous action, a virtuous action, but lack the spiritual dimension. In order to qualify as a spiritual action it must be performed with (a) a conviction that one is doing it not *just* out of brotherly love and compassion (though these feelings ought also to be involved) but rather because there is a transcendent demand that one act compassionately, and (b) a conviction that what one is doing is not merely of passing help to some needy individual but of lasting significance as according with the "higher purpose" of the world. The former of these requirements is fulfilled, in the case of the traditional Jew, by his knowledge that the Torah instructs us to be compassionate, to give alms. The latter requirement is fulfilled by reflecting that the Torah represents the fulfillment of the divine plan for the world. In almsgiving, therefore, one is taken out of the realm of the particular and beyond the practicalities of the present, relating the immediate, limited deed to the infinite, spiritual purposes of God. This is the function of what we may, without prejudice to its objective truth, refer to as the "Torah-myth," the story of the laws, received by Moses from God, reaching down to us at the present time through an unbroken chain of authorized interpreters; the story enables us to "spiritualize" our deeds by relating them to a divine Source. The story, at its minimum, is simply our way of expressing our conviction of the ultimate ontological significance, the numinous overtones, of our deeds.

One who is conscious of *performing a mitzvah,* therefore, as opposed to one who is simply "doing a good deed," links himself with the transcendent Source of his morality—in a word, *spiritualizes* his action. Torah is thus the link between God and man, a link mediated and progressively defined by a recognizable historical process. It enables one to whom God does not speak *directly,* as He spoke to Moses, to share, in a guided and controlled manner, the same sense of acting in accordance with God's will and purposes.

II. CHARACTERISTICS OF THE SOURCE

The spirituality of the Torah is the spirituality of its Source.

What, apart from numinosity, can we ascribe to this Source?

Morality, we have already indicated. For our present purpose we need not involve ourselves in speculation as to whether morality is rooted in God or is an eternal, independent value. Suffice it to say that our perception of God, *through Torah,* is thickly intertwined with our sense of right and wrong. Thus one of the most agonizing situations in which the Torah-oriented Jew finds himself is one in which there appears to be a conflict between a rule of *halakha* and a deeply cherished moral principle—a problem to which we must return later.

Compassion, concern for man's well-being, is a frequently stressed aspect of the spiritual Source; as we have seen, "at Sinai He revealed Himself as an old man steeped in compassion. . . ." God's revelation of the Torah to Israel is seen as His supreme act of love, and Sinai as a marriage feast. The very multiplicity of the commandments is adduced by the Mishnah as evidence of God's care for Israel: "Rabbi Chananya the son of Akashya said: 'The Holy One, blessed be He, wanted to give Israel opportunity to be worthy (in His eyes); therefore, He gave them a profuse Torah with many commandments.' "[7] God acts here as a loving father surrounded by adoring children; the father does not really need anything from his children, but keeps them happy by "inventing" little jobs for them to do so that he can reward them without their feeling embarrassed about getting something for nothing. Constantly, when citing Scripture, the Talmud says *rachamana amar,* "The Merciful One says . . ." or rather, as this is an Aramaic expression, and in Aramaic the verb *rchm* usually means "love," "The Loving One says. . . ." This love is essentially a redemptive act of God.[8] He has given Torah to Israel to enable them to overcome sin. As Rabbi José put it: "Israel received the Torah in order that the Angel of Death should have no power over them";[9] or, in the words of R. Johanan in the name of R. Benaah, "Happy are Israel, for so long as they are engaged in Torah and charity the *yetser* (evil inclination) is under their control, and they are not controlled by the *yetser.*"

The *joy* of Torah is a prominent aspect of the Jew's experience of fulfilling the *mitzvoth,* and part of the relationship with its transcendent Source. "The Holy One, blessed be He, gave the Torah to Israel and rejoiced." Of Rabbi Eliezer and Rabbi Joshua who studied Torah together with such love and intensity that "fire came down from heaven,"[10] it is related that "the words (of Torah) were as joyful as the day they were given at Sinai." This joy *at the source* of the *mitzvoth* is expressed at their fulfillment through *simcha shel mitzvah,* a value stressed by though not unique to the Hassidic movement. *Simcha shel mitzvah* is not merely the satisfaction one gets from a "job well done," or the happiness of knowing that one has benefited society or another individual, though such emotions are not to be despised. *Simcha shel mitzvah*, however, is a sense of being linked, through Torah, to the joyful Source of all being. It is a spiritual, rather than a material, satisfaction. Hence the rabbinic dictum *mitzvoth lav lehanot nitnu* (the *mitzvoth* were not given for pleasure),[11] which, far from denying the joy of performing a *mitzvah,* is in fact a rule with the effect that if, for instance, a man is bound by a vow not to benefit from another, the other may perform a *mitzvah* for him, e.g., sound the *shofar* for him; the "pleasure" of listening to the *shofar* at the New Year is *simcha shel mitzvah,* a transcendent, spiritual joy, rather than a material one, hence not proscribed by the vow. Such joy is the appropriate mood for prayer, for "One should not commence prayer in a mood of sadness, indolence, hilarity . . . but through *simcha shel mitzvah.*"[12] When Rabbi Ila'a saw Ulla off to Babylon he instructed him to draw attention to R. Bruna by a specially effusive public greeting, for "He is a great man; he rejoices in *mitzvoth.*"[13]

Following hard on the heels of the *joy* of the *mitzvah* is *care* in its performance. The orthodox Jew never appears as ridiculous in the eyes of his detractors as when fussing over some apparently trivial detail of ritual performance. Likewise, the lover never appears as ridiculous in the eyes of the unbesotted as when tearing himself apart psychologically to decide whether his beloved would prefer to receive exactly this or that service or gift from his hands, when we all think we know that it wouldn't make a jot of difference to her one way or the other. But we don't care for her all that much; he does. So, to the orthodox Jew, *dikduk b'mitzvoth,* exactitude, perfect correctness in the performance of *mitzvoth,* is one of the highest religious values, and he is hardened to putting up with a great deal of ridicule from his less orthodox friends for this particular form of demonstration of his love of God. Did not the great Maimonides say that one's love of God should be like love of a woman?[14] But a lover has a duty to study carefully the needs of the beloved, to assess her priorities, and for this Maimonides provides a comprehensive code. One must know—and the true student of Torah knows this—that it is not only apparently but in reality foolish to work oneself into a state of anxiety about the shape of a petal on one rose in a bouquet while at the same time overlooking the beloved's need for food, drink, raiment to wear, and the touch of the caressing hand. The *pseudo*-orthodox, who will fuss inexorably about minutiae of ritual law while cheating at business, failing to address themselves to the real needs of society, and mumbling uncomprehended set formulae instead of praying, are, if we are very charitable toward them, in the category of the foolish lover.

Beauty is of the essence of the Source experience, and is crystallized in the bidding of the *halakha:* "Make yourself beautiful before Him through *mitzvoth;* make a *beautiful* succah, a *beautiful* lulav, a *beautiful* shofar."[15] The midrash on the Song of Solomon affords the rabbis an opportunity both to pay tribute to the beauty of women and to use it as a pointer to the transcendent beauty of Torah: "Just as the breasts are the glory and beauty of a woman, so were Moses and Aaron the glory and beauty of Israel."[16] Of Jerusalem, the geographical link between God and mankind, an early rabbi asserts: "Ten portions of beauty came into the world; Jerusalem took nine, and the rest of the world one."[17] The Zohar declares: "In time to come, the Holy One, blessed be He, will make the bodies of the righteous as beautiful as that of Adam in the Garden of Eden."[18] The steps of the pilgrims wending their way to Jerusalem are praised for their comeliness;[19] Rabbi Ishmael is lauded for assisting poor girls to improve their appearance.[20] Note how the transformation of beauty into a transcendent Torah-value leads not to the negation of ordinary earth-based beauty but to its enhancement. One dedicates beauty to God not by abstaining from its appreciation in this world but by seeking to experience it through the *mitzvoth*—the beautiful sabbath-table, the beautiful Synagogue, and not least the beauty of the human form and human relationships as expressed in those activities and situations approved by the *halakha;* for indeed the power of beauty is so great that it is only too easily exploited by the *yetser hara,* the evil inclination.

Three other values are expressed through the *halakha* and characterize the spirituality of its Source: blessing, purity and holiness. All three are distinctively religious values, absent by and large from secular life, so that it is difficult to convey their meaning within the normal vocabulary of contemporary English. Here again one sees the effectiveness of the *mitzvah*-concept; for in itself it constitutes a language, and a child who is brought up on *mitzvoth,* however inadequate his spoken vocabulary, learns quickly to appreciate the meaning of blessing, purity and holiness, for he acquires command of the act-vocabulary, namely the *mitzvoth,* which can say so much more than mere words.

Already, analyzing the Source-spirituality of Torah, of *halakha,* we have numinosity, morality, compassion, redemption, joy, beauty, blessing, purity and holiness, all focused through *mitzvah* into the simple, practical terms of ordinary life. We are beginning to understand.

III. THE WAY

Torah is the totality of the Way, both that which can be formulated as rules and principles and that which cannot.

Mitzvah is the specific action viewed as the Word of God.

Halakha is the rule-system—"a *halakha*" is a specific rule, or a specific application of a rule.

Halakha includes not only rules but principles. For instance, there are rules as to liability for damage inflicted by persons or their agents or their property on other people or other people's property. There are also principles regarding equality of people before the law, equity, unjust enrichment, the application of *darke shalom,* pursuit of peace, to the law, and so on; in the "religious" sphere we have come across the principle "*mitzvoth lav lehanot nitnu,*" the *mitzvoth* were not given for pleasure. There are also indications as to "weighting," the priority to be given where there is *prima facie* conflict between one rule and another, one principle and another, or between rule and principle.

Halakha is far-reaching, ranging from civil jurisprudence to Temple ritual, from agriculture and tithes to marriage and divorce, from festival procedure to personal hygiene, and impinging even upon ethics and philosophy. But the more *halakha* enters the realms of ethics and philosophy the less it is resolvable into a rule-system, the more one calls for personal judgment, inspired judgment, the *ruach hakodesh,* holy spirit, which alone gives life to the whole system.

For there is no law-system in the abstract. One could not feed the *Shulkhan Aruch,* a medieval halakhic Code, into a computer and use it as a *dayan,* a judge—though a *dayan* may well be happy to use such a computer to store and process information. *Halakha* is a living system, functioning only through its authorized judges and interpreters, who participate in its actual *creation.* "When a judge makes a decision in absolute truth," taught Hiyya bar Rav of Difti, "it is as if he were a partner of the Holy One, blessed be He, in creating the world."[21] The words *din emet la-amito,* "in absolute truth," imply more than integrity on the part of the judge, far more than mere correctness in handling a rule-book; the demand is that the judge act in conformity with the *whole* Torah, that his spirit be united with Torah for whose fulfillment the world was created.[22] If, and only if, the *dayan* can act in this way, his decision carries the stamp of authority entrusted to Moses, for ". . . scripture, Mishnah, laws, Talmud, Tosefta, *aggada,* even that which any faithful disciple was to say in the presence of his master—all were related to Moses at Sinai."[23]

Early in the second century it was definitively established that halakhic decisions were in the hands of human judges; for the Torah *lo bashamayim hi* (Dt 30:12) was "not in heaven."[24] A fascinating, if non-halakhic, illustration of this principle is found in the course of a discussion between two third century Palestinian rabbis, Abiathar and Jonathan, about some detail of fact in the story of the concubine of Gibeah (Jgs 19). Rabbi Abiathar happened to meet the prophet Elijah (who had ascended to heaven in a fiery chariot some centuries previously) and asked him what God was currently doing. "Studying the passage about the concubine of Gibeah," replied Elijah. "Then how does He interpret it?" "He says, 'Abiathar my son says so-and-so, and Jonathan my son says so-and-so,' " returned the prophet; and the *gemara* epitomizes: "Both are the words of the living God."[25] So the rabbis of each generation participate in the creation of Torah, and God on high is pleased to concur with their views—but only if they are men of humility and piety and learning through whom the holy spirit can breathe.

A debate[26] erupted in Israel recently in connection with the long-standing attempt to introduce Jewish Law into the law-system of the State, an attempt which, though it has some backing from religious quarters, is essentially an expression of national revival analogous with the revival of the Hebrew language; both, for use in a modern, secular State, need to be updated and, in particular, stripped of their religious layers. Against this, Izhak Englard, Professor of Law at the Hebrew University, has powerfully argued that there is no way in which *halakha,* as such, *can* be incorporated into the Israeli legal system. Even if a particular statute were to be formulated entirely on the basis of rabbinic law it would, by incorporation in the law of the secular State, *ipso facto* cease being rabbinic law, for the law would be detached from the normative system within which the procedures for its application and the resolution of its problems lie. In Englard's words, "The immediate social aim of settling a conflict of human interests does not always require a direct reference to the ultimate metaphysical end of man's existence."[27] If I may simplify the argument, Englard is stating, as we have done already, that the essence of the system of *halakha* lies in its transcendent source; its judges and interpreters take their authority from this source. Although the words of a statute of a secular state may coincide with those of a Torah statute they can be no more than a "bleeding chunk" detached from its life-source. Englard is right to point out that such "chunks" are no longer *halakha;* but I do not agree that it follows from this that openness to traditional influences is a bad or inappropriate thing for Israeli law.

There is no Torah, no *halakha,* apart from people—God pointedly abstained from handing the Torah to his ministering angels[28]—and "people" means first and foremost the judges and interpreters—*dayanim,* rabbis—in each generation. But the people of Israel as such have some part in defining the *halakha* within the parameters set by the authorized judges and interpreters; the Codes—that of Moses Isserles (1525–1572) and Josef

Karo (1488–1575) rather more than that of Maimonides (1135–1204)—abound in instances of *minhag,* customary law. *Minhag* adds a further dimension to the spirituality of *halakha,* for it contributes a sense of involvement with history, not just the formal history of the law but that of the whole Jewish people; and this history, as experienced through the *halakha,* is not a list of secular events but the dialogue of the people with God, a continuation of the Holy Scriptures themselves. On one occasion, when the Temple still stood in Jerusalem, the great Hillel found himself unable to answer a question about the procedure for the Passover sacrifice; confidently, he counseled the sages to bide their time and observe what the people actually did: "Let Israel alone; if they are not prophets, they are the sons of prophets!"[29] Happy is the leader who is so sure that his people walk in the footsteps of the Men of God!

IV. MEN OF THE WAY

"Rabbi (Judah the Prince) said: 'I succeeded in understanding the Torah only because I saw the back of Rabbi Meir's neck.' Rabbi Yochanan and Rabbi Simeon ben Lakish said: 'We were able to understand the Torah only because we saw Rabbi's finger emerge from his glove.' "[30] Whatever the obscure incidents that underlay these observations the meaning is clear enough: Rabbi, and then his two disciples, want to bring home to us that Torah must be understood from life, from people whose lives are lives of Torah; Torah is not an abstract science to be acquired from books alone. The same Rabbi Yochanan—a third century Palestinian sage—states the principle very clearly: *gadol shimushah yoter milimudah,*[31] the service of the Torah (i.e., attention to the personal needs of the sages) is greater than its learning (is of more value than actual study).

The sage is the avatar of Torah, and although the cult of the individual was rarely taken to excess in Judaism before the rise of Hasidism, the *talmid chakham* has traditionally been the most respected person in the community. Certainly, a dimension of the halakhic experience is provided by contact with the man of learning and piety. The "guru" may not always be a living one—there is even a hasidic sect, the Braslaver, whose "Rebbe" "passed on" early in the nineteenth century, though they still turn to him as their model and mentor. Rabbi Joseph Dov Soloveitchik, who is not a hasid, writes so beautifully of his relationship with the great sages of the past that I must quote a lengthy section of the deeply moving work on the "search for God" he composed (in Hebrew) in memory of his wife:

> I recall, when I was young, I was a loner, afraid of the world. . . . It seemed as if everyone made fun of me. But I had one friend—don't laugh—the Rambam (Maimonides)!
>
> The Rambam was a regular visitor in our house. . . .
>
> Father's lectures were given in the hall of my grandfather's house, where my bed was placed. I used to sit on my bed and listen to Father's words, and he was always talking about the Rambam. . . . He would open the *gemara,* read through the section to be studied, and say . . . "This is how it is explained by the Ri and the Tosafot; now let's look at the Rambam and see how *he* explains it." He would always discover that the Rambam explained it differently, and not in accordance with the obvious meaning. He would say . . . as if personally complaining to the Rambam: "Rabbenu Moshe, why did you do this?" . . . He would lean his head on his clenched hand, deep in thought. Everyone would be silent, so as not to disturb his thoughts. After a long time he would slowly raise his head, and begin: "Gentlemen, let us see, now. . . ."
>
> I understood not a word of the subject, but two impressions fixed themselves in my innocent young brain: (1) The Rambam was surrounded by opponents and "enemies" who wanted to harm him; (2) Father was his only defender. Who knows what would have happened to him without father? . . .
>
> (Sometimes) I would go broken-hearted to my mother: "Mother, Daddy can't explain the Rambam! What shall we do?" "Don't worry," Mother would say. "Father will find an answer for the Rambam. And if he can't, perhaps when you grow up you will find an answer for the Rambam. The main thing is to keep on learning Torah, and to enjoy it and let it excite you." . . .
>
> This was no golden daydream of a young child. It was a psychological and historical reality which even today lives in the depths of my soul. When I sit and learn I find myself at once in the company of the wise men of tradition, and our relationship is a personal one. The Rambam is on my right, Rabbenu Tam on the left, Rashi sits in front and explains, Rabbenu Tam fires questions, Rambam makes decisions, Raavad criticizes. All of them are in my little room. . . . They look at me with affection, join in reasoning and *gemara,* support and encourage me like a father.
>
> The learning of Torah is not merely a didactic exercise . . . but the powerful expression of a love that crosses the generations, a marriage of spirits, a unity of souls. Those who hand down the Torah meet in one inn of history with those who receive it.[32]

Such is the spirituality of the *halakha* to those who immerse themselves in learning!

Both in this work, and in his *Ish Hahalakha,* which is a philosophical portrait of his grandfather, Rabbi Hayyim Soloveitchik of Brisk (1853–1918),[33] Joseph Dov Soloveitchik tries to elucidate the distinguishing characteristics of the "halakhic man." In its simplest terms, this is what he says. The world knows two types of personality. On the one hand, there is the distinctively religious man, who emphasizes the "mystery" of the world, the depth of its meaning, its ultimate significance; on the other hand, there is the man of science, who would strip the world of its mystery and seek to explain it in simple terms and even to control its workings. These two types of men reflect a duality in the world itself, for the world has both aspects. The "man of halakha" bridges the gap, provides the synthesis required by the dialectic between religion and science; though in many respects a "man of religion," sensitive to the voice of God and the profundity of life, he is at the same time a "man of science," able to express himself in simple, practical, non-mystical terms.

One does not have to share Soloveitchik's philosophical views to appreciate the value of his presentation of the *experience* of the life of *halakha,* and of the way in which the halakhic man has, so to speak, succeeded in confining the transcendence of the spirit within the boundaries of space and time.

But it must be admitted that on occasion the "spiritual force" within the *halakha* breaks from its confinement. Of Jonathan the son of Uzziel, Hillel's greatest disciple, it is related that when he sat and learned Torah so great was the fire of his spiritual passion that if a bird flew overhead it would burst into flame.[34]

V. JEWISH MYSTICISM

What of the Jewish mystic, the kabbalist? Is not his soaring spirit far too noble and free and holy and spiritual to be trammeled with the burden of discipline imposed by the *halakha?* Surely, as would seem to be indicated by Martin Buber,[35] the ecstasy of the "I-Thou" meeting, the basis of moral decision, is on each occasion such a unique experience that it cannot give rise to rules and laws. Is not true spirituality necessarily antinomian?

The answer to these questions is quite simply "No!" Buber grossly misrepresented Jewish mysticism by severing it from *halakha.*

Kabbalah, as represented in the Zohar, the Lurianic writings, and mature Hasidism, is totally and essentially bound up with *halakha;* it grows out of *halakha,* it supports *halakha,* it elucidates *halakha.* Josef Karo himself was a mystic, believing himself "possessed" from time to time by a spiritual mentor, the Mishnah—the fundamental classic of the *halakha*—in "person." Enter a hasidic Synagogue when the *Omer* is counted—watch the ecstatic fervor, the swaying from side to side, the cries from the heart, as the hasid counts the *Omer,* concentrating his mind on the interlinking aspects of the ten *Sefirot* which govern that particular stage in the progress from Pesach to Shavuot.

To read Buber, one would think that Rabbi Nachman of Bratslav was no more than a weaver of fantastic spiritual tales. Throw aside this image, and immerse yourself (nothing less will do) for some months in the study of *Likkute Moharan,* in which his principal teachings are presented. You will discover that Rabbi Nachman's real "Torah" is an elaboration, in what we may loosely call theosophical terms, of *halakha* as represented in the *Shulkhan Arukh.* What is the mystical significance, the "inner meaning," of washing the hands before meals, then again at the end of the meal? Why does a marriage agreement have to be committed to writing? Why is it that whereas the Jewishness of a child is determined according to its mother, whether it is Cohen, Levi or Israelite goes according to the father? These are the sort of questions on which Rabbi Nathan, summarizing his master's teachings, discourses; and in this, he is simply following the lead of the great kabbalists of earlier generations. There is no cleavage between Jewish mysticism and *halakha;* indeed the former presupposes the latter.

But kabbalah does add a further dimension to the "spirituality of *halakha.*" For its devotees, it provides a means of turning both the study of the Torah and the observance of the *mitzvoth* into experiences enriched by mystical awareness, by consciousness of the aspects of the Godhead as presented in the kabbalistic writings. It is to the credit of Hasidism that it succeeded in bringing something of this fundamentally esoteric approach within the reach of the ordinary Jew—but only, be it said, of the ordinary Jew in the course of his observance of the *halakha.*

VI. SPIRITUALITY AND THE CONTEMPORARY JEW

So far, a happy picture has emerged of the halakhic Jew, immersed in the study and fulfillment of the *mitzvoth,* absorbing the multiform radiation of the divine spirit. How far does this idyllic picture portray the life of real people?

The key to its effectuation lies in the *yeshivah,* the institute within which young men—most of them not pursuing a rabbinical vocation—are introduced to traditional Torah-study. The peculiarly devout intensity of *yeshivah*-study is not matched by the university student, for it involves an act of faith, and a commitment to study as an approach to God—not through mystery, but through the practicality of the *halakha;* prayer, study and action are united.

From the *yeshivah* the ideal spills out into the daily life of the people. The home reflects the values of the *yeshivah,* and many men continue *yeshivah*-type study throughout their lives, attending *shiurim,* learning together with a close friend, their friendship deepened by this spiritual bond. Some belong to a worldwide fraternity such as the "Daf Yomi," members of which commit themselves to learning a page of Talmud each day; wherever and whenever they meet, they are ready to converse about the "page of the day."

But there are tensions, clouds within the halcyon sky. Some of these, rightly faced, are the stimulus to future growth, for Torah is never complete. Any list of such tensions must be somewhat tendentious, and I offer the following as no more than an adumbration of my personal experience.

(1) The most uncomfortable tension felt by those who would like to emulate the "man of *halakha*" is that between individual conscience and the precise norms of *halakha.* This is at its most acute in those fields where contemporary thought on moral and ethical issues stresses rights which traditional *halakha* ignores or minimizes. A major instance of this is the rights of women; one adds insult to injury by patronizing talk of women being "equal but different" so long as, for instance, they are excluded from the *yeshivot* and all higher rabbinic learning not on the grounds of individual lack of aptitude but purely because of their sex.

(2) *Halakha* at its best is responsive to changing social and economic conditions, for though it has no legislative body it possesses a built-in flexibility of interpretation. Tension is caused by the reluctance of the orthodox leadership to make use of this flexibility. The confrontation with Conservative Judaism is one result of this tension, and has led to orthodox reaction into still greater inflexibility.

(3) "Happy is the man who is constantly apprehensive; but he who hardens his heart will fall into evil" (Prov 28:14). But one can be too apprehensive, too worried about the finer detail of *halakha* to notice the great issues of life which it also handles. One can become so bound up, for instance, in the *halakha* about the slaughter of birds of food that one does not find time to consider the less intricate if more important *halakha* about loving one's neighbor. The rabbis, from talmudic times onward, have frequently complained about this imbalance among the superficially observant. In the Lithuanian *yeshivot* in the 1890's a controversy broke out as to

whether the study of Musar (ethico-philosophical writings) might be introduced into the curriculum.[36] Undoubtedly the call for the introduction of Musar was a response to the sort of imbalance I have indicated; the opponents correctly, if disingenuously, argued that Musar study was superfluous for *yeshivah* students, for a proper study of *halakha* as presented in the Talmud *included* everything that need be known about ethical behavior.

(4) There is a constant tension between the world of the Talmud, which tends to center on fifth century Babylonia, and that of the contemporary world. This ought to be a stimulus to development of rabbinic thought, but is sometimes allowed to become an excuse for withdrawal into a private world, or a self-imposed ghetto.

I must give the final word to Joseph Dov Soloveitchik, who has done more than anyone in our time to demonstrate the ideal of the "man of *halakha*":

> The public reading of the Torah is not simply for the purpose of instruction; it is a meeting with God, like that of our fathers at Sinai. Each reading is a new Revelation, a reliving of that wonderful scene at the foot of the mountain burning in flame.[37]

The experience of the *halakha,* whether in learning or in fulfillment, is the experience of Sinai.

The spirituality of the *halakha* is the spirituality of its Source.

NOTES

1. J.Z. Lauterbach, transl. and annot., *Mekilta de-Rabbi Ishmael* (Philadelphia: JPS, 1949) on Exodus 15:3.

2. Cf., e.g., the opening of *De Creatione.* To be fair to Philo, he does in fact say in the opening of his *Life of Moses* that Moses was "according to others only an interpreter of the sacred laws."

3. The allusion here is to a rabbinic comment on Genesis 9:27, suggesting that the "beauty of Jephet," i.e., some aspect of Greek culture, might dwell in the tents of Shem, i.e. among the Jewish people. Cf. TB *Megillah* 9b.

4. H. Danby, transl. and annot., *Mishnah* (Oxford: Oxford Univ. Press, 1933), Sanhedrin 10:1.

5. TB *Sanhedrin* 99a.

6. H. Sperling, M. Simon, transl., *The Zohar* (London: 1931–1934), Nefesh Hahayyim 4:10.

7. *Mishnah* (see note 4), end of Makkoth.

8. The Zohar spells out particularly clearly the redemptive aspect of Torah, and it is a central theme in later Kabbalah.

9. TB *Berakoth* 5a.

10. TJ *Hagigah* 2:1.

11. TB *Rosh Hashanah* 28a.

12. TB *Berakoth* 31a.

13. TB *Berakoth* 9b. Some read "Eleazar" in place of "Ila'a."

14. Maimonides, *Yad-Ha-Hazakah* (or *Mishne Torah*), Teshuva 10:3.

15. TB *Shabbath* 133b.

16. H. Freedman, Maurice Simon, transl. and ed., *Midrash Rabbah* (London: Soncino Press, 1939), Shir Hashirim Rabba 3.

17. TB *Kiddushin* 49b.

18. *The Zohar* (see note 6) Genesis 113.

19. TB *Hagigah* 3a.

20. TB *Nedarim* 66a.

21. TB *Shabbath* 10a.

22. Cf. M. Rosenbaum, A.M. Silberman, eds., *Pentateuch with Rashi's Commentary* (London: Shapiro, Vallentine, 1929), Genesis 1:1.

23. *Midrash Rabbah* (see note 16) Vayikra Rabba 22:1. There are several variant versions of this aggada. Cf., for instance, TB *Abodah Zarah* 5a, where Adam has the vision.

24. The *locus classicus* for this concept is the debate between Rabbis Eliezer and Joshua, recorded in TB *Baba Meziah* 59b.

25. TB *Gittin* 6b.

26. An excellent presentation, in English, of some of the important material in the debate is to be found in Bernard S. Jackson, ed., *Modern Research in Jewish Law* (Leiden: E.J. Brill, 1980). This is Supplement One of the Jewish Law Annual.

27. *Op. cit.*, p. 24.

28. TB *Shabbath* 86b.

29. TB *Pesahim* 66a.

30. TJ *Bezah* 5:2; cf. TB *Erubin* 13b.

31. TB *Berakoth* 7b.

32. Joseph D. Soloveitchik, *Ish Hahalakha* (Jerusalem, 1979), chapter "Uvikashtem Misham"; the quotation runs from page 230ff.

33. *Ibid.*

34. TB *Sukkah* 28a.

35. On Buber and the *halakha* cf. Marvin Fox, *The Philosophy of Martin Buber* (London: Library of Living Philosophers, 1967), essay on "Buber's Moral Philosophy." Cf. also my article, "Martin Buber and Orthodox Judaism," in *European Judaism* 12, No. 2 (Winter 1978).

36. Cf. Lester Eckman, *The History of the Musar Movement* (New York, 1975), e.g., p. 134.

37. Joseph D. Soloveitchik, *op. cit.* (see note 32), p. 227.

5.
Liturgy: Function and Goal in Christianity

Mark Searle

Scholars have discussed at length the relationship between Christian liturgical forms and the matrix of Jewish prayer and worship out of which they sprang.[1] The question is a difficult one due to the problems of establishing with any degree of certainty the patterns and content of Jewish worship in the first century of the Common Era. Nevertheless, every Christian participating in common prayer is confronted with vestiges of our common past in such words as *Amen* and *Alleluia,* in the proclamation of readings from the Common Testament as Word of God, in the cycle of the seven day week, in the annual observance of Pascha and Pentecost. The rooting of the two great sacraments of Baptism and Eucharist in prior Jewish practice is also unarguable, even if the precise nature of the connection is still a matter of conjecture and debate.[2] Christian Baptism is generally thought to have derived from the practice of John the Baptizer and more generally from the baptismal movement which flourished along the Jordan Valley. The Christian Eucharist obviously claims the Last Supper of Jesus with his disciples as its point of origin, but the practice of ritual meals, even apart from Passover, was not uncommon among pious Jews of the time. The central prayer of the Eucharist has been shown to derive from the *berakoth* tradition (though what this meant at the time is disputed), while the use of Isaiah 6:4, or *Sanctus,* is thought to have derived from its use (as *Kedushah*) in the synagogue. Finally, the importance attributed to the gathering of the faithful for proclamation of the Word and for worship—a gathering whose Greek name, *ekklesia,* gave the Christian movement its name—was largely the result of the way the new community saw itself as being in line with the great assemblies (*Kahal*) of the people of Israel.

Given the subsequent development of Christian worship, as it moved into different cultures and developed a bewildering variety of ritual traditions, it is not surprising that Christians by and large should have lost sight of the common source of their liturgies in Jewish worship. For this reason, it is important to acknowledge our common heritage at the outset, even if the specific focus of this article does not permit us to develop the subject further. Still, it must also be admitted that even if we were to discuss the Jewish roots of Christian liturgy we would also be required to account for the distinctiveness of Christian worship and to indicate how this distinctiveness originates in the person and work of Jesus himself. In the present context we are addressing the question of the function and goal of Christian worship in general, rather than looking at the origin and evolution of worship forms. This requires us to focus on what is original in Christian liturgy, namely the confession of Jesus as the Christ and the new set of relationships with God, one another and the larger world which results from that confession.

At this point it is as well to remember the conviction shared by Jews and Christians about the importance of history and about the importance of remembering the past if we are to be faithful to the God who shapes our future. For Jew and Christian alike, God remains ultimately transcendent, for all his closeness; ultimately mysterious, for all his historical self-revelations. To talk of worshiping this God is to talk of entering into the presence of the Holy One. Like Moses, we have to learn on what ground we stand. Thus, from age to age, Christians have come to perceive the goal and function of their worship differently, as each successive generation of believers takes up the tradition, lives it, and passes it on. But the tradition itself is more than any one generation does and the mystery is more than any one set of images and concepts can conceive. For this reason, it would seem best to discuss the goal and function of Christian worship in terms of different historical periods and then to attempt a theological synthesis, always bearing in mind that the sketch of each period can only hint at the religious genius of the believers who prayed and worshiped at that time and that the synthesis itself is not so much an attempt to describe the mystery as to distill some of the perennial characteristics of the Christian understanding of worship.

I. AN HISTORICAL PERSPECTIVE

1. Christian Origins

The newness of Christian worship vis-à-vis Judaism depended entirely and from the beginning (even when the relationship of the new community to Jewish traditions was painfully problematic) upon the conviction that the God of Abraham, Isaac and Jacob had acted anew to reveal himself to humanity, and to save, in the person of Jesus of Nazareth. The implications of this conviction were not immediately obvious, so that the New Testament writings echo internal dissension over the problem of how much continuity with the past was compatible with the radical newness of God's intervention in these "last times." Ritual observances such as circumcision, fasting, the distinction between clean and unclean, participation in Temple and synagogue worship, and the keeping of the Sabbath were all subjects of painful deliberation in the early years. But the Gospels reveal clearly that if the decision was made to break with such observances in the new age, such a decision was only possible because Jesus himself had opened the way for such freedom from the Law and, in so doing, had acted upon the authority of the God he called "Father."

It would be misleading, however, to think of Jesus or the early Church as replacing one ritual system with another. Indeed, it would be truer to say that early Christianity was characterized by a lack of ritual worship, by its radical secularization. The general picture of Jesus that emerges from the Gospels shows him breaking with ritual worship, rather than simply spiritualizing it in the tradition of the prophets.[3] Thus Christianity's break with Jewish worship and its adamant refusal of any kind of compromise with pagan worship was not merely a stage in its search for its own identity, but a result of the conviction that, in the new order of things inaugurated by God in Jesus, religious ritual in all recognized senses of the term was quite simply overtaken. In its place was the worship which consisted of a life lived in the obedience of faith, which meant in conformity to Jesus' own total surrender of his life to God for the salvation of the world.

One significant indication of the radical secularization of worship which resulted from the belief that in Jesus the promised "end times" had arrived is the almost systematic avoidance of cult terminology in the Christian vocabulary, or, more precisely, the metaphorical use of such terms to refer to Christian realities. Apart from occasional references to pagan religions and to the Jewish Temple, the term "sacrifice" is used in the New Testament to describe the death of Jesus, the Christian life of obedient faith, collections taken up for the poor, and the selfless expenditure of life and energy for the sake of the Gospel. In short, Christian worship was understood to consist entirely of serving God and one another without reserve, as Jesus had done. Similarly, terms like "worship" and "liturgy" are used of Christians, not to describe their cultic acts but to indicate the quality and direction of their lives. As Ferdinand Hahn remarks:

> The terminological evidence means not only that any cultic understanding of Christian worship is out of the question, but also that there is no longer any distinction in principle between assembly for worship and the service of Christians in the world.[4]

As Hahn also points out, the only term with possibly cultic overtones that is regularly applied to Christian behavior in a literal sense is that of assembling (*synerchesthai, synagesthai*).[5] The purpose of such assemblies is well summarized in the Acts of the Apostles as fellowship, teaching, prayer and the breaking of bread, or Eucharist. But such gatherings were characterized by their domestic setting and their comparative informality, while initiation into the community was a relatively simple affair carried out in rivers or streams or the domestic bath. Thus, while the assemblies of the early Christians were not totally devoid of ritual (some degree of ritualization being inseparable from any form of communal interaction, especially when the interaction centers on *la vie sérieuse*), they were nevertheless far removed from the rubrical elaborations of contemporary religious practice or of later Christian generations.

Moreover, what ritual forms did exist were themselves totally permeated with the sense of the transformation of the *saeculum* which had been initiated through the death and resurrection of Jesus and the eschatological outpouring of the Spirit which characterized the present age. In other words, the irruption of God's eschatological activity in and through the person of Jesus was seen as destroying any separation of sacred and secular activities, places or persons: the only separation left was between belief and unbelief. Yet paradoxically, as David Martin has argued,[6] to maintain the new secularism, sacred rituals had to be developed; to attain the new universalism, a new particularism was required; the development of an egalitarian society of brothers and sisters required the emergence of a class of "fathers." In short, for the new order to be sustained, it had to elaborate structures of ministry and authority, boundaries of affiliation and nonaffiliation, specific sacred rituals which would point to the sacredness of all human activity. This is precisely what occurred.

In the first generations of the Church, then, the goal and function of Christian liturgy were identical with the goal and function of Christian life itself, and not sharply distinguished from the rest of the community's life in its forms. Moreover, the goal and function of Christian life were in turn identified with the goal and function of the life and death of Jesus himself, as this was understood: the making present on earth and in human form of the rule and Kingdom of God. It was to embody and express submission to "the God and Father of our Lord Jesus Christ," and this to the same end as Jesus himself had lived and died: for the glorification of the Father and the salvation of the world. These two ends were inseparable insofar as salvation consisted in acknowledgment of God as newly manifested in the life and death of Jesus, while acknowledgment of what God had done for us in Jesus was expressed not only in the "sacrifice of lips" but in the mutual love and concern of the believers.

Finally, the resurrection and exaltation of Jesus meant that he continued to be with his Church, the body of which he was the head, and continued to exercise his mediatorial role between the Father and humanity. The Epistle to the Hebrews, for example, expresses this in terms of the abolition of the Temple priesthood and the establishment of Jesus as the unique and universal high priest who represents his fellow human beings before the throne of God, offering his life as a once-for-all yet ever-valid sacrifice, the source of divine blessing for all humanity. Here, in the imagery of the Temple liturgy, we find the same convictions being expressed as they surface elsewhere in the New Testament: that God's eschatological rule and Kingdom had broken into history in the life and death of Jesus; that the death of Jesus was the definitive and victorious consummation of God's history of revelation and salvation; that Christ, through the working of the Spirit, continues to be with his people, especially when they gather in his name. Thus, the early Church did not so much celebrate the past as remember the past in order to understand the realities of the present, while anticipating the future and visible return of Christ to establish the Kingdom of God "in glory" thereby bringing history to an end.

2. The Constantinian Church

The year 313, which marked the beginning of Constantine's enfranchisement of Christianity in the Roman Empire, serves as a convenient starting point at which to begin talking about a new style of Christianity. The term "Constantinian Church" refers to the Christian Church first as emancipated and then as the established religion, although some of the developments of the "Constantinian Church" had already begun in some places before 313. The new situation of Christianity as the state religion, while a source of anxiety to many and a sign of the victory of the cross to others, actually wrought profound changes in the spirit and ethos of the Christian community which were symptomatically manifested in the liturgical celebrations. A series of changes took place which reflected the new situation: the move from house to basilica, from small face-to-face groups to large, comparatively anonymous congregations, from domestic table to permanent altar, from earnest informality to solemn ceremony, from a leadership which was indistinguishable from the community in terms of marital status, occupation, dress to a ministerial class which gradually distanced itself from the people in life-style, social status and by becoming full-time religious professionals, "sacred persons."[7] In the fourth century the Church experienced the ambivalence of massive growth and of legal establishment, but it also underwent more subtle accommodations. By joining forces with the secular powers and hoping to "Christianize" them, the Church inevitably compromised its critical role: instead of proclaiming the demise of earthly power structures in face of the advent of the Kingdom, the power structures were to be made to serve the Kingdom and hence to be given a new lease on life. This, together with the adoption of Greek thought on much the same principle, resulted in a transmutation of the Christian imagination where the Kingdom of God was concerned. It has been said that the substitution of Greek thought categories for Hebrew ones included a preference for thinking in spatial rather than temporal terms. Thus the Kingdom of God ceased to be thought of seriously as a future cosmic event which was already at work and which subverted the present socio-political order. Instead, its transcendence of the world-as-we-know-it came to be imaged in spatial terms, as a parallel, if "higher" world, with which contact could be made only by discrete acts of intervention from above. This imaginal shift was furthered by the fourth-century controversies over the divine and human natures of the Christ, where, despite the moderate, middle-of-the-road character of the final conciliar consensus, the net result was in practice an exaggerated sense of the divinity and "other-worldliness" of Jesus.[8] Since his presence in the liturgy had been a fact of the Church's faith from the very beginning, the result was the increased "sacralization" of the liturgical rites, their description as "holy and awesome," the screening off of the "sanctuary area" and the altar from the gaze of the common people, and an emphasis on the holiness and other-worldliness of the liturgical ministers themselves—a series of developments which are quite obvious in Eastern Christianity, but which also affected the West, if more slowly and more subtly. The function of the liturgy was to open a door into the heavenly city and to participate in the worship of heaven.

3. *The Medieval Church*

The Middle Ages, by definition, were constituted by the fusion of Roman civilization, Christian religion and the energies of the Frankish and Germanic tribes. In the course of this fusion, all three elements underwent profound changes, and many of these changes, and emergent new forms, were manifest in the liturgies of the Christian West.[9] The "sacralization" of the rites, already underway, was further enhanced by the failure to translate the liturgy into the vernacular languages. Thus literate clerics (clerks), versed in Latin (which had become the language of law and diplomacy, as well as of liturgy), became even more of a caste apart. The eucharistic liturgy came to be envisaged as the work of the priest alone, with or without popular attendance. Church buildings began to reflect the new imagination, becoming sacred sanctuaries where the priestly work was done on a multiplicity of altars, rather than gathering places for the worship of the Christian community. The emphasis on the Godhead of Jesus tended to displace him from his mediatorial role, particularly in a feudal society where hierarchical systems of patronage and fealty were deeply ingrained. The "distancing" of Jesus from his people (his image appeared on the tympanum of the church entrance, seated in judgment) left a gap which was filled by the ministrations of the hierarchical Church, equipped to teach, rule and sanctify, and by Mary and the saints whose intercessory functions loomed large throughout this period. All this was fueled by anxiety about one's personal salvation which intensified in the later Middle Ages and tended to turn Christianity into an arsenal of meritorious works and a vast system of spiritual patronage, operative in this world and beyond. The liturgy tended to be seen primarily in terms of offering propitiatory sacrifice and dispensing saving grace for the benefit of individual Christians to allow them to negotiate the perils of this world and to make it safely into the Kingdom of heaven. The development of psychological awareness which characterized the high Middle Ages fostered a heightened sense of individualism[10] (probably not unconnected with anxiety about salvation) and an affectivity which found its outlet in realistic representations of the passion and death of Christ and in highly colorful legends of Mary and the saints. Given that the liturgy itself remained substantially unaltered, being in Latin and in the exclusive domain of the clergy, it was inevitable that the popular religious life of the period grew increasingly remote, both in form and in spirit, from the practice of the liturgy. Insofar as the liturgy played a role in people's consciousness, its function and goal was virtually reduced to providing Christian people, living and dead, with the "grace" they needed to be delivered from eternal damnation when they came before the judgment seat of God.

4. The Modern Church

The liturgy, envisaged as we have described, was clearly open to abuse as well as somewhat remote from the understanding of Christian worship in New Testament times. By the early sixteenth century, the situation had become quite intolerable,[11] and it was Martin Luther who, in 1517, finally launched that attack on the whole system, riddled with superstition and abuse, which came to be called the Reformation. The divisions which this reform occasioned and the different kinds of reform which resulted have characterized Western Christianity and its liturgies up until the twentieth century, while the Churches of the East remained almost entirely unaffected by the upheavals in the West.

(a) *The Protestant Reformation.* Luther launched his attack on the sacramental "machinery" of salvation in the name of faith. It was faith in the Word of God revealed in Jesus Christ which meant salvation, not the operations of the cleric-dominated sacramental system. The implications of this fundamental principle were interpreted differently by different movements within the Protestant reformation,[12] but characteristic of them all was an immediate revision of the liturgical tradition in accord with what was considered to be the teaching of the New Testament and the practice of the early Church. The general result was an overall emphasis on the reading of the Scriptures in the language of the people and on preaching, to the extent that the sacramental principle, which held the presence and action of Christ in the actions of the liturgy, was played down and in some instances entirely rejected. The function and goal of Christian worship, in the general perspective of the Protestant Reformation, was the enlightenment and edification of the people so that they might thankfully acknowledge what God had done in Jesus Christ and live accordingly.

(b) *The Catholic Reformation.* Those European churches which took a more conservative approach to reform matters and retained their ties to the Church of Rome undertook joint reforming programs of their own while rejecting the doctrinal and liturgical excesses of the Protestant churches. The Council of Trent served to reaffirm medieval doctrinal positions on such matters as the sacrifice of the Mass, the reality of Christ's presence in the Eucharist, the efficacy of sacramental rites, the legitimacy of retaining the Latin language, and the powers invested in the priest in virtue of ordination. On the other hand, the Council also condemned the abuses of superstition and simony which had provoked the reform movement in the first place and commissioned an overhaul of the liturgical books which was left to the papacy to carry out. The result, in Roman Catholicism, was a genuine revival of liturgical worship, though it was characterized by conservative retention of a medieval theology of liturgy, a new preoccupation with fidelity to rubrical details, and a devotionalism which, while amazingly fruitful, tended to be dominated by an individualistic psychology and by moralism. The hallmarks of Catholic life of this period were a highly methodical approach to growth in holiness and a corresponding activism which found its outlet in carrying out devotional exercises on the one hand and in works of charity on the other. Indeed, attendance at the liturgy and reception of the sacraments tended to be regarded as acts of personal devotion and edification which would fuel both the inner life of prayer and service of one's neighbors. They were understood less as sacramental signs than as causes of grace, and hence the continuity between liturgical worship and the Christian life as lived worship was lost sight of. The devout believer passed from the profane world of secular life to the sacred world of private prayer alone or in common, but the two worlds remained distinct and the secular world was ever regarded as a hostile arena of dangers and temptations.

5. *The Contemporary Church*

The twentieth century, building on the renewal of theological and biblical studies which resulted from the development of historical criticism in the nineteenth century, has seen a remarkable return to the sources of Christian worship.[15] The divisive issues of the sixteenth century have largely been transcended in theology, while the liturgical practices of the different Christian churches of the West show increasing similarity as theological agreement and a common respect for the normative character of the early worship tradition have come to prevail. Among the chief elements of this recovered tradition must be mentioned the renewed awareness of the assembled community as the true "celebrant" of the liturgy of the Church, a new and more informed appreciation of the role of the Scriptures proclaimed as Word of God in the assembly, and the restoration of the community Eucharist as the center and high point of common worship. Protestants have become increasingly aware of the sacramental dimensions of worship, while Catholics have shown remarkable appreciation of the scriptural and ethical elements in a liturgy they had for too long been content to regard as a divine operation. From the early days of the liturgical movement, a concern for social justice was typical of many of its leaders, but for perhaps the majority of Christians the intrinsic connection between the liturgy of the Church and the worship of daily life, such as characterized the early Church, remains problematic.

II. CHRISTIAN LITURGY—A THEOLOGICAL SYNTHESIS

1. God-in-Christ

Christians share with Jews and Muslims the conviction that the God we serve is one God and that there is no other. Whether that God be named Yahweh, Allah, Father, Ground of our being, or any of the other names with which believers call upon this One, we know that the One is beyond any name that can be named and that all that is comes from the One, is sustained in being by the One and must return to the One. Christians share with Jews and Muslims, too, the conviction that this unnameable God, for all the divine transcendence and incomprehensibility, is a God who has overcome the distance between divinity and humanity, has shown a will to engage us in a real relationship of love, and, to that end, has disclosed the divine presence in human history. Certain historical events are commonly recognized as having more than historical significance, as being acts of God reaching out in love to save humankind. Certain historical individuals are recognized as prophets and prophetesses who have "lived with God" and acknowledged as interpreting authoritatively the revelatory events which must otherwise have remained submerged in the stream of mundane historical existence. Certain writings, purporting to be authentic testimony to the self-disclosure of God in human events, are commonly acknowledged as divine Scripture, serving to bring remembrances and promises to each successive generation as if it were the first.

At the heart of Christianity lies the conviction that this one God, far transcending all naming and knowing, is disclosed as a personal presence at the heart of the world in the person, life and death of Jesus of Nazareth, who "was born of the Virgin Mary, suffered under Pontius Pilate, was crucified, died and was buried" and "on the third day rose from the dead," to be "seated at the right hand of the Father." Henceforth he stands in judgment upon all humanity: "he will come again in glory to judge the living and the dead." The Christian faith reposes on the conviction that this Jesus was the Messiah of God, that in him this One became visible, articulate and historically effective in human form, so that to look upon Jesus is to witness the ultimate anthropomorphism: the Transcendent incarnate in the life and death of a man. It is an anthropomorphism which depends for its revelatory and salvific power upon the maintaining of paradoxes which defy human understanding and overwhelm the believer with a sense of the divine wisdom surpassing human invention: the paradox of the *Shekhinah* dwelling in the son of a carpenter, of divine power manifest in the scandal of one who was arrested and crucified, of salvation for the whole human race coming through one who was apparently unwilling to save himself. The liturgy of the Christian churches tends to celebrate the intervention of God in Christ in ringing affirmations of the Word made flesh, and in triumphant celebration of the victory of God in the death and resurrection of Jesus and in repeated prayer that the Spirit of God, manifest in the life of Jesus and destroying death by raising him to life, might animate and enliven us in our turn. Yet the paradoxes which cluster together under the concept of incarnation continue to haunt us, even—perhaps especially—in the celebration of the liturgy.

The very intractability of the Word of God incarnate in Jesus Christ has always provoked and continues to provoke theological attempts to expound that mystery, attempts which, as we have suggested in our brief historical sketch, both derive from and in turn have shaped the encounter with that mystery in the liturgy of different ages and different Christian traditions. Nevertheless, two constants remain in all Christologies which are axiomatic for all Christian liturgy: the initiative which God takes toward the human race (revelation and salvation) and the response which this requires from us (the obedience of faith expressed in life and worship). The fulcrum of both these moments is human existence itself: *caro salutis cardo,* as Tertullian expressed it.[16] This is true of Christ, the Word made flesh, whose human existence both revealed the saving power of God and itself constituted the source and paradigm of human responsiveness, and of the Church which constitutes a continuing embodiment of divine presence and activity in the lives and actions of believing communities. Thus incarnation is more than a way of talking about God-in-Christ; it is a continuing principle of the Christian life itself. It is synonymous with sacramentality.

2. Sacraments

The term "sacrament" is most commonly used by Christians today to refer to those forms of Christian liturgy which most immediately and explicitly mediate a saving encounter between God and the believers through Jesus Christ in the Church. But this restricted meaning, as it applies, for example, to the sacraments of Baptism and the Eucharist, itself depends upon a broader concept of sacramentality.

In the widest sense, anything and everything may be seen as sacramental insofar as the universe itself is seen as creation, as a work of God whose goodness and love it expresses and reflects. More specifically, the events of human history in which God has gradually revealed himself as one who is engaged with us and has a plan for humanity may themselves be spoken of as sacraments. Above all, Jesus Christ himself, as the culmination and fulfillment of that plan manifest and enacted in the shape of a human life, is properly spoken of as the sacrament of God. To speak of sacrament, therefore, is to point to ambivalence. It is to speak of a perceptible reality—in the created universe, an historical event, a personal presence and activity—which serves to disclose the presence of the Holy and to mediate a saving encounter. This encounter in turn is experienced as engagement. (The classical Latin *sacramentum* referred to a military oath and was used to translate the Greek term *mysterion:* the two together suggest the double dynamic of divine initiative and human commitment discussed above.)

For Christians, Jesus Christ is the primordial sacrament,[17] in the light of whom and in dependence upon whom all other sacraments may be recognized. Talk about the divine and human natures of Christ (and all the paradoxical statements of Christology and soteriology) is an attempt to grapple with his sacramentality, maintaining both the reality of God's salvation disclosed in his life and person and the reality of his own human engagement with the God he called "Father." In Jesus we see most clearly that divine initiative and human response are not, properly speaking, two separable moments, but that the divine initiative is disclosed in the very act of submission and that his human obedience is inseparable from the self-disclosure of God which informs it. Hence, the whole personality and life of Jesus, who he was, what he did and said, are understood as sacramental.

The "Christ-event," above all his suffering and death and resurrection, is both a disclosure of what God is like (the kind of God we are involved with is the kind of God revealed in the fidelity and powerlessness of the crucified Jesus) and a revelation of what the acknowledgment (worship) of such a God involves. The death of Jesus is, therefore, both sanctification in an active sense (the effective revelation of God's redeeming love) and in a passive sense (the consecration of human existence to the glory of God). It is God being for us and we being for God. It is the overcoming of alienation between God and his human creation through a surrender which is completed in the restoration and perfection of the self that surrenders. God is glorified in Jesus who hands over his life, but that self-alienation is (paradoxically, again) the discovery of the true self, the gift of God we call "resurrection" and "eternal life."

"What was visible in Christ," said St. Leo the Great (†460), "has passed over into the sacraments of the Church."[18] What was visible in Christ, we have argued, was the pattern of God's initiative and transforming human engagement. These have passed over into the sacraments of the Church as their underlying pattern and *raison d'être:* sanctification and worship—divine action and human transformation under the impetus of that action—to the glory of the One who acts. But to speak of the "sacraments of the Church" means more than to speak of things belonging to the Church, for sacraments are, in this context, ritual actions, i.e., activities engaged in by the Church as gathered congregation. From this perspective, it is clear that the liturgical actions of the Church are sacramental insofar as the celebrating community is itself sacramental. Jesus did not simply announce the Word of God; in all he was and did, he *was* the Word of God. Similarly, the Church does not simply celebrate the sacraments, but is itself in a prior sense a sacrament of God's activity in the world. The gathered congregation is a sacramental sign of the presence of God and of his saving Word and grace, sharing the ambivalence common to all sacrament-signs, namely, the ambivalence of being an empirical psycho-sociological phenomenon *and* the disclosure of the presence of God. All the activity of the Church, to the degree that it is a faithful response to the Word of God, is potentially sacramental. But the liturgical activity of the Church is most specifically sacramental insofar as it is in her worship assemblies that her true character and ultimate *raison d'être* as sign and presence of divine-human encounter is most immediately and specifically manifest.

The connection between the person and work of Christ and the reality of the liturgical assembly goes beyond that of simple imitation of Christ or the carrying out of specific rituals which he mandated or instituted. For Christians, Christ remains the sole and continuing mediator between God and the human race, the head of the new humanity brought into being by God through the reconciliation he worked in and through Christ. The dispositions of the historical Jesus, namely his total surrender to the will of the Father which enabled him to serve as the most adequate instrument of the divine will, remain forever valid and operative. It is this which is suggested by the exaltation of Jesus and by his representation as eternal High Priest, living forever to make intercession for those who approach God through him (Heb 7:24ff; 10:8ff). Christ is also the goal of Christian worship, insofar as the effect of engaging in the liturgy of the sacraments is to transform the believers more and more into the likeness of Christ in his own surrender to the Father and in his exaltation, his being delivered out of death, by the power of God. Thus the person and work of Jesus governs the past, present and future of Christian liturgy.

Nevertheless, while Christians speak not only of God acting in the sacraments of the Church, but of the sacraments themselves being the actions of Christ among us (for the Church sees itself organically united with him as his Body), yet it is also clear that Christians live now in the absence of Christ. More exactly, the presence of Christ to his Church as mediator of God is effected through the release among us of the Spirit of God. That same Spirit which was at work in Jesus as the principle of divine activity in revelation and salvation is now operative in the personal lives and especially in the congregational assemblies of those who, through the operativity of that Spirit, have come to believe in Jesus as the mediator between God and humanity. Thus, in the ancient formula, Christian prayer and worship is offered to the Father through Jesus Christ in the power of the Holy Spirit. *The Apostolic Tradition of Hippolytus* (c. 215 CE) concludes its prayers: "Glory be to you, Father, with the Son and with the Holy Spirit in the holy Church, now and always . . ."[19] thereby suggesting that it is the presence of the Spirit in the community of believers which makes it the primary sacrament of which specific sacramental rituals are particular articulations.

The work of the Spirit in the Church is, as we have already suggested, to transform the community more and more into the likeness of Christ in his obedience unto death. The most revealing and characteristic moment in the life of Jesus was his passion and death, his total surrender to the Father who alone could save him out of death (Heb 5:7). This "paschal mystery" of the transformation of death into new and immortal life, of suffering into glory, of submission into exaltation constitutes the only approach to God there is. The operations of the Spirit in the liturgy are toward the realization of this mystery in our lives—to draw us into the sacrificial death of Jesus, that we might share his acceptance by God and be reconciled with the Father. The language of Spirit in liturgy, as in the Scriptures, is the language of talk about God's activity in us and among us bringing us to faith and all that that implies for acknowledgment, commitment, confession and transformation.

Every sacramental liturgy, whether Baptism or the Eucharist or Marriage, thus celebrates the paschal mystery and engages believers in it in ways appropriate to their situation. The readings, prayers and gestures of each rite mediate, in ways appropriate to the circumstances, the "life and death" encounter with God in Christ. They are not simply *about* the paschal mystery as encounter with God. Through the operation of the Spirit they draw us into that encounter. The sacraments not only signify, but they effect what they signify for those who participate in ways appropriate to each particular rite and to their role in its celebration.

3. Sacraments of Faith

Baptism is the sacrament of faith; the Eucharist is called the mystery of faith. The two terms are synonymous. Indeed, all Christian liturgies are sacraments of faith insofar as they both express and engender faith. This faith, which the Roman Canon identifies as the faith of Abraham, is defined by Vatican II in Pauline terms as "the obedience of faith . . . an obedience by which man entrusts himself entirely to God, offering the full submission of intellect and will to God who reveals."[20] The Roman Canon identifies this as the faith of Abraham, of whom the Epistle to the Hebrews says that "he obeyed when he was called, and went forth to the place he was to receive as a heritage; he went forth moreover not knowing where he was going" (11:8). Such faith found its fulfillment and perfection in Jesus "who inspires and perfects our faith. For the sake of the joy which lay before him he endured the cross, heedless of its shame. He has taken his seat at the right hand of the throne of God" (12:2).

The faith that the sacraments are meant to express and engender, then, is the faith which is required to draw near to God through Christ, the faith which Christ himself manifested in his own suffering and death, that total obedience and self-surrender to God of which death is both the symbol and the reality. Baptism is baptism into the death of Jesus in the hope of sharing his resurrection (Rom 6:3–5). To celebrate the Eucharist is to proclaim the death of the Lord, to identify with his broken body and with the pouring out of his life. Marriage is the celebration of "love stern as death," whereby two people lay down their lives for the other, that in their dying new life may spring forth. Anointing of the Sick brings to expression and acceptance the God-given opportunity to transform one's suffering into the commitment of faith, so that the power of God might be revealed once again in human weakness. Penance confronts us with the false gods we serve and with the illusions of pseudo-salvation which we substitute for faith in God; it calls us to abandon our willfulness and to surrender to the God who alone can save us from death. Ordination to church leadership implies modeling the priesthood of Jesus which was exercised in his fidelity unto death and in his selfless concern to establish the Kingdom of God, without counting the cost.

The faith which is expressed and engendered through the ritual of the Church's liturgy is, in the first place, the faith of the individual believer. The reading of the Scriptures, the formulae of prayer and creed, the songs, sermons and exhortations all serve to enable the believer to remember the works of God and to become more profoundly aware of who he is and who he will be. But faith is not only a matter of hearing and believing. It is a way of being in the world, a stance toward life. The ritual actions and sacramental gestures rehearse such fundamental attitudes as are compatible with faith: kneeling in penance and submission, standing before the presence of God as his people, casting the shadow of life-through-death upon oneself with the sign of the cross, discovering the radical newness of Christian identity in the baptismal immersion, discovering the dimensions of the community of believers—and the sacrifice which brings it into existence—in the eucharistic breaking of bread. The sacraments require faith, but we need the ritual repetition and the encounter with the same ultimate mystery in significant dimensions of life, because faith always co-exists with un-faith. As disciples, we are in course of learning what this faith is that requires us to move away from the city of the Chaldees, to suffer the uncertainties of the desert and the ignominy of the cross. Regular participation in the sacraments of faith is necessary for all the disciples of Jesus.

Yet the faith which the sacraments express is more than the sum of the beliefs and attitudes of the particular congregation. The sacraments express the faith of the Church, also known as the Tradition. While such Tradition is certainly expressed in the history of Church doctrine and practice, it cannot simply be identified with these. The Tradition is the total identity and *raison d'être* of the Christian Church. Doctrinal, moral and devotional traditions are ways in which this deeper Tradition has come to conscious expression and articulation, but they point beyond themselves to the mystery of the person who acts and speaks, to the mystery of God's continuing involvement with the human race in Jesus Christ which is the ultimate source of the Church's identity. It is this identity, shaped upon the matrix of the paschal mystery of Jesus' death and resurrection, which constitutes the faith of the Church, a faith which is expressed, but never adequately or exhaustively, in creedal statements, ecclesiastical institutions and devotional life. The challenge to the believers who participate in the liturgy of the Church is to move ever more deeply into the mystery of the Church's faith-existence, her Tradition.

That faith-existence of the Church is in turn, as we have already suggested, to be identified with the faith of Jesus himself who entrusted himself entirely to God in death as in life. This faith of Jesus remains: in the Book of Revelation, he is portrayed as a lamb that has been slain and yet is standing, suggesting the enduring validity of the sacrificial death of Jesus and its eternal acceptance by God (5:6). Thus the death and exaltation of Jesus remain forever as our way of access to God, and the Church remains Church to the degree that she lives out this inner mystery of hers and does not herself betray it in history. Thus the faith of Jesus is constitutive of the faith-identity of the Church, and the faith-identity of the Church makes it possible for believers of every generation to surrender themselves to God in the faith of Jesus and to discover God's power to save.

Clearly, such a life of faith cannot be limited to the weekly or even daily hour of worship. The paschal mystery is not something limited to the sacraments, or even to Christian life. When we speak of the universal significance of Christ's death, of his being the sole mediator between God and humanity, we are not suggesting that God has arbitrarily narrowed salvation down to one man, or set up prescriptions for salvation which the vast majority of the human race have never been informed about. The reverse is true. The paschal mystery is the name for the paradox which all great religions recognize and which Jesus summarized in the words, "he who saves his life will lose it" (Mt 10:39). Christians believe that the pattern of God's dealings with humankind, laid bare in the life and death of Jesus of Nazareth, are true and valid for all humanity; there is no other way to life except that which Jesus opened up. Christians see themselves in relation to the world in much the same way as they see liturgy in relation to Christian life: not as distinct and apart, but as pointing back to the ultimate nature of all human existence. The liturgy is the source and summit of the Christian life insofar as it reveals the gift of God's gracious and saving presence at the heart of human life and draws us into a ritual rehearsal of the conversion of life which is the hallmark of a life lived in that presence.[21]

4. Liturgical Spirituality

The spiritual life has been defined as one of relating to one's relationships. The human person is shaped by a network of relationships: to oneself, to significant others, to society at large, to the material universe, to time which both contextualizes these relationships and ultimately (as a journey toward death) threatens them. To live a spiritual life is to do more than simply live *in* these relationships; it is to relate to the relationships and thereby to become aware of their meaning and their mystery.

Given the richness of the Christian religion, it is inevitable that different cultures and different ages have emphasized different aspects, finding more relevance in some Christian images, doctrines and practices than others and thereby developing different traditions of spirituality. There are traditions which are dominated by vivid awareness of the historical events of the life of Jesus, while others tremble before his divine exaltation. Some have developed the cultus of Mary and the saints; others have given the emphasis to Scripture. Some have been more aware of the divinizing power of the Spirit in the Christian life; others have been overwhelmed by a sense of human sinfulness and impotence. Hence it is possible to speak of different spiritualities, or schools of spirituality, in Christianity. Liturgical spirituality, however, is not another school or tradition, so much as the acknowledgment that it is in the liturgical celebrations of the Church that we continually come up against the mystery in its incomprehensible wholeness. A spiritual life that allows itself to be shaped by the liturgy is one which relates to the relationships of life under the guidance of the kind of relationships which the liturgy itself exemplifies. It is impossible to develop this point fully here, and the following are simply brief indications of such a spirituality.

(a) *Relationship to the Self.* A person becomes a Christian through Baptism whereby he or she is associated in faith with the dead and risen Christ. Baptism celebrates and confers a new God-given identity, expressed in the language of "forgiveness of sins," "adoption," "regeneration," "enlightenment." The gift is also vocation, a call to die to one's egocentric existence and to begin to live for God in the love and service of one's fellow human beings. This vocation to a life of commitment is affirmed and empowered in the sacrament of Confirmation and continually renewed, week by week, in the Eucharist. The sacrament of Penance reflects the lifelong struggle to be true to the new self and to overcome the rear-guard revolt of the ego. The surrender of one's life to God in the acknowledgment of one's inability to save oneself is particularly vivid in the Anointing of the Sick and the liturgy of Christian death.

(b) *Relationship to Others.* "None of us lives to himself, none of us dies to himself," wrote Paul (Rom 14:7). Human existence is co-existence and Christian life is essentially common life. We are called and saved, not as individuals, but as a people. God's salvation is for the human race as a whole, not just as an accumulation of individuals, and the Church understands herself as a first sign of a new beginning of human life lived under the rule of God. The Church, strictly speaking, becomes Church when the faithful assemble in the *ecclesia* (congregation), and her liturgy is not the action of some individuals on behalf of others so much as a celebration of the whole body. In the weekly assembly, the Christian becomes aware of his place in the scheme of things, as part of something larger that God is working in history and in this place and time. The practice of common prayer, addressing God as "Our Father," the performance of common gestures, the asking of forgiveness from one another, the exchange of the kiss of peace and, above all, the sharing of the one bread and the one cup at the weekly Eucharist are meant to shape our Christian consciousness about the quality and meaning of our relationships with one another and our fellow human beings.

(c) *Relationship to the Material World.* Christian liturgy makes use of the material creation in many different forms: bread, wine, oil, water, incense smoke, lighted candles, fire, beeswax, wood, stone, fine linen and woven cloths, flowers and plants, iron and brass. In the liturgy, natural elements are taken up in their pure or manufactured state to become objects which mediate relationships between the community and God, among the believers themselves. The use of these things in the liturgical rites points to the need for, and the possibility of, the redemption of the non-human universe. As stewards of creation, we can implicate creation itself in our sinful alienation from God by using it in ways which divide us from one another, whether by producing instruments of war or by unrestrained consumption at the expense of the poor. Our vocation, however, is to allow creation to find its intended fulfillment in becoming a medium of communication and hence of communion between human beings and a sacrament of our common Creator. As Eucharistic Prayer IV suggests, through our faithful remembrance of God even silent creation finds a way to praise its Creator. The acknowledged sacramentality of material things in the liturgy thus opens our eyes both to the sacramentality of creation itself and to the just use and distribution of the world's wealth.

(d) *Relationship to Time.* The liturgy of the Church has its own calendar which stakes its claim, among all the other calendars by which we live, upon our use of time. There is the weekly rhythm of the Sunday assembly, the great seasons of Christmas (with Advent) and Easter (with Lent and Pentecost), and the annually recurring feasts of salvation and the commemoration of the saints. There is the daily cycle of prayer, hinging on the celebration of morning Lauds and evening Vespers with their hymns and psalms, readings and prayers. The function of this liturgical timetable is to keep remembrance alive, lest we forget who we are and what we are called to be. For the Christian, as for the Jew, to remember is to be, to forget is to cease to be. To remember the acts of God is to be obedient to his purposes in history. To cease to remember is to begin to live by another story, to condemn oneself to irrelevance and to oblivion before God. Thus, liturgical celebrations are not simply commemorations of the past, but a means for renewing and deepening our awareness of the divine history in which we are involved. Time is redeemed and the tyranny of death is broken when past, present and future are ritually redescribed as the story of God in Jesus Christ, in such a way as to catch us up in that history-in-the-making.

5. *Liturgy and Eschatology*

The eschatological dimension of Christian liturgy is probably the dimension least recognized even by Christians themselves. The liturgy is widely regarded as remembrance of the past and sanctification of the present, but its essential orientation toward the future has generally been overlooked with the abandonment of that expectation of an imminent end to the world which characterized the first Christian generation. Nevertheless, the liturgy still teaches us to pray insistently for the coming of the Kingdom of God and for the full realization of the divine plan for the reunification and restoration of all things under the rule of God, which Christ is seen as having initiated and which the Spirit of God is bringing about. The eucharistic liturgy, both in the dynamism of the great Eucharistic Prayer, moving from past to future, and in the ritual eating and drinking which is a symbol of the great banquet in the Kingdom, is the central bearer of eschatological promise, a role in which it is supported particularly by the liturgy of daily prayer and by the liturgy of Advent, with its readings from the prophets and from the apocalyptic passages of the Gospels.

Two connected developments have led to the loss of eschatological tension in Christian life. The first is the reinterpretation of the *eschata* in terms of individual death and judgment. The second, its correlate, is the transposition of the Kingdom of God in the Christian imagination from the temporal dimension (as the goal of history, exerting a tug upon the present) to the spatial dimension (as another, higher world). Whatever the cultural causes of this shift, the results have been serious. In the first place, the switch of focus from the end of the world to the end of the individual life means that the values of the Gospel were interpreted more as an individual rule of life than as a continuing critique of the socio-political kingdoms of this world. Sin was viewed as a matter of personal failure and the structural and collective manifestations of evil were overlooked. Secondly, what was true of the Church's relationship to society at large also came to be true of the inner life of the Church, namely that sin and conversion were matters affecting the lives of individual Christians but not the life of the Christian community as such. Individuals sinned, but the Church was holy. The loss of eschatological tension thus deprived the Church of its collective conscience and thereby opened the way for accommodation with other unholy collectives and for the unconscious projection of the Church's own faithlessness and guilt upon outsiders.

There are indications at the present time that the renewal of the liturgy, together with a more profound theology of history and a more vivid sense of the Church's own historical conditioning, may be bearing fruit in a growing eschatological realism in Christianity.[22] This, in turn, will reawaken the prophetic understanding of the inseparable connection between liturgy and social justice.

III. CONCLUSION

In the case of liturgy, as in other areas of human life, it is important to remember that unreflective behavior precedes and gives rise to theoretical reflection. In other words, the practice of Christianity is in every way prior to theology and the worshiping life of generations of believers is more than putting liturgical theology into practice. Indeed, the liturgy itself is *theologia prima,* an immediate, existential word addressed to and about God in prayer. As such it not only precedes but also transcends any reflective, theological account of it: what we are and what we do is more than we can adequately account for.

Nevertheless, having said that, it is still necessary to be able to offer some description, however provisional, of the goal of Christian liturgy and of how that liturgy functions in service of that goal. In summary of the preceding, it may be said that the goal of Christian liturgy is the glorification of God through the transformation of the human race. This transformation is always in process. It involves the transformation of individuals, but cannot be restricted to the individual, for nothing less than the shaping of human history is at stake in the intervention of God in our world. The liturgy functions by drawing us simultaneously into the ambit of God's transforming Spirit and thereby enabling us to acknowledge God as our God. It functions as a provisional, sacramental realization of its goal, the Kingdom in which everything will be subjected to Christ: "Then the Son himself will also be subjected to the One who made all things subject to him, so that God may be all in all" (1 Cor 15:28).

NOTES

1. Besides references given below, the following represent a significant sample: W.O.E. Oesterley, *The Jewish Background of the Christian Liturgy* (Oxford, 1925); L. Bouyer, *Liturgical Piety* (Notre Dame, 1955), pp. 23–37, 99–128; Bo Reicke, "Some Reflections on Worship in the New Testament," in *New Testament Essays (Essays in Memory of T.W. Manson)* (Manchester, 1959), pp. 194–209; G. Delling, *Worship in the New Testament* (Philadelphia, 1962); C.W. Dugmore, *The Influence of the Synagogue upon the Divine Office* (London, 1964); J. Jeremias, *The Prayers of Jesus* (London, 1967); B.H. Jones, "The Quest for the Origins of the Christian Liturgies," in *Anglican Theological Review* 46 (1964) 5–21; W. Rordorf, *Sunday* (Philadelphia, 1968); N.D. Mitchell, "Jewish Liturgy in the Talmudic Period," in *Resonance* 4 (1969) 18–44.

2. On Baptism: G.R. Beasely-Murray, *Baptism in the New Testament* (London, 1963); J. Delorme, "The Practice of Baptism in Judaism at the Beginning of the Christian Era," in A. George, ed., *Baptism in the New Testament* (London, 1964), pp. 25–62; S. Legasse, "Baptême juif des prosélytes et baptême chrétien," in *Bulletin de Litérature Ecclesiastique* 77 (1976) 1, 3–40; B.E. Thiering, "Inner and Outer Cleansing at Qumran," in *New Testament Studies* 26 (1980) 2, 266–277. On Eucharist: G. Dix, *The Shape of the Liturgy* (London, 1945); K.G. Kuhn, "The Lord's Supper and the Communal Meal at Qumran," in K. Stendahl, ed., *The Scrolls and the New Testament* (London, 1958), pp. 65–93; J.P. Audet, "Literary Forms and Contents of a Normal Eucharistia in the First Century," in *The Gospels*

Reconsidered (Oxford, 1960); M. Thurian, *The Eucharistic Memorial* (London, 1961), Part II; L. Bouyer, *Eucharist* (Notre Dame, 1968); L. Ligier, "From the Last Supper to the Eucharist," in L. Sheppard, ed. *The New Liturgy* (London, 1970), pp. 113–125; T. Talley, "From *Berakah* to *Eucharistia:* A Reopening Question," in *Worship* 50 (1976) 115–137.

3. Ferdinand Hahn, *The Worship of the Early Church* (Philadelphia, 1973), studies attitudes to worship in the New Testament using historical critical methods. For a different approach, cf. G. Delling, *op. cit.*

4. Ferdinand Hahn, *op. cit.,* p. 38.

5. *Ibid.,* p. 36.

6. David Martin, *The Breaking of the Image* (Oxford, 1980), p. 26.

7. Cf. J.A. Jungmann, *The Early Liturgy to the Time of Gregory the Great* (Notre Dame, 1959); Th. Klauser, *A Short History of the Western Liturgy* (London, 1969); P. Rouillard, "From Human Meal to Christian Eucharist," in *Worship* 52 (1978) 5, 425–439 and 53 (1979) 1, 40–55.

8. For the effects of the Christological controversies, cf. J.A. Jungmann's classic study, *The Place of Christ in Liturgical Prayer* (New York, 1965).

9. A.L. Mayer, *Die Liturgie in der europaeischen Geistesgeschichte* (Darmstadt, 1971). For the broader context, cf. David Knowles and Dimitry Obolensky, *The Middle Ages* (New York, 1968).

10. C. Morris, *The Discovery of the Individual, 1050–1200* (New York, 1972), sketches the cultural shift that so influenced later medieval Christianity.

11. For a survey of the problems, cf. J.A. Jungmann, "The State of Liturgical Life on the Eve of the Reformation," in *idem, Pastoral Liturgy* (London, 1962), pp. 64–79. For a fuller catalogue, cf. A. Franz, *Die Messe im Deutschen Mittelalter* (Darmstadt, 1963).

12. Cf. Y. Brilioth, *Eucharistic Faith and Practice, Evangelical and Reformed* (London, 1930); E. Underhill, *Worship* (New York, 1957).

13. R. Theisen, "The Reform of the Mass Liturgy and the Council of Trent," in *Worship* 40 (1966) 565–583.

14. On the liturgy in the Baroque period, cf. L. Bouyer, *Liturigical Piety, op. cit.,* pp. 1–9; also J.A. Jungmann, *Pastoral Liturgy, op. cit.,* pp. 80–88.

15. O. Rousseau, *Histoire du mouvement liturgique* (Paris, 1945); E.B. Koenker, *The Liturgical Renaissance in the Roman Catholic Church* (Chicago, 1954); M.J. Taylor, *The Protestant Liturgical Renewal: A Catholic Perspective* (Westminster, 1963).

16. Tertullian, *De resurrectione carnis,* 8. CSC, *Series latina,* vol. 2, 931.

17. This term is borrowed from E. Schillebeeckx whose classic work, *Christ the Sacrament of Encounter with God* (New York, 1963), is the inspiration of much of this section. For some reservations on Schillebeeckx's approach, cf. G. Wainwright, *Doxology* (New York, 1980), pp. 70–73.

18. Leo I, *Tractatus* 74:2, CSC, *Series latina,* vol. 138A, 457.

19. B. Botte, ed. *La Tradition Apostolique* (Liturgiewissenschaftliche Quellen und Forschungen) vol. 39, 16:20.

20. "Dogmatic Constitution on Divine Revelation," in Austin P. Flannery, ed., *Documents of Vatican II,* 5, p. 752. Cf. Rom 1:5; 16:26.

21. Cf. Karl Rahner, "Secular Life and the Sacraments," in *The Tablet* (1971) 236–238, 267–268; *idem* "What Is a Sacrament?" in *Theological Investigations* 14 (1976) 135–148.

22. For example: J.L. Segundo, *The Sacraments Today* (Maryknoll, 1974); J. Mateos, *Beyond Conventional Christianity* (Manila, 1974); H. Schmidt and D. Power, eds., *Politics and Liturgy* (New York, 1974); T. Balasuriya, *The Eucharist and Human Liberation* (Maryknoll, 1979); M. Searle, ed., *Liturgy and Social Justice* (Collegeville, 1980).

6.
The Rites of Initiation and Christian Spirituality

Ronald Lewinski

Christian churches take their mandate for initiation from Christ's command: "Go, therefore, and make disciples of all the nations. Baptize them in the name of the Father, and of the Son, and of the Holy Spirit" (Mt 28:19). Christians have understood baptism as a necessity, recalling the risen Christ's words: "The man who believes in it (good news) and accepts baptism will be saved" (Mk 16:16). While the biblical roots for baptismal practice may be held in common in Christian churches, the development of baptismal rituals and theology has varied greatly.

The initial practice of initiation was apparently very simple and carried none of the ritual embellishments or catechetical requirements we presently assume. In the Acts of the Apostles we find Philip meeting an Ethiopian eunuch on the road, reading from the prophet Isaiah. After a discussion they approached some water in which Philip immediately baptizes the eunuch with apparently little preparation or ritual (Acts 8:26–40). We also find a jailer in the Acts of the Apostles who in an apparently brief encounter with prisoners, Paul and Silas, was baptized together with his whole household, again with apparently little preparation or ritual (Acts 16:25–34).

If in fact there appears to be a lack of ritual and catechetical structures in regard to early Christian initiation, it is not an indication of laxity or pastoral indifference in the early Church. Those who chose to join the Christian community were received into the community more spontaneously. They were gradually drawn into the Christian way of life by their association with Christians, which, if the account of community life in Acts 2:42–47 is any indication, was very intensive, demanding and personal.

Catechetical preparation for new Christians began to develop very quickly, however, especially when the original band of Jesus' followers were no longer living and eyewitness accounts of Jesus' deeds and teachings were no longer available.

The *Didache* (c. 150 CE) could well be the first catechism that was used in the formation of new Christians, especially with its description of the "two ways": a Way of Life and a Way of Death. The *Didache* bears strong traces of Jewish roots, reminiscent in particular of earlier Jewish teaching found in Deuteronomy 30:15.

By the third century we find in the *Apostolic Tradition* of Hippolytus (c. 215 CE) an emerging set of rubrics and rites that surround the basic baptismal bath. The catechumens, or candidates for baptism, are to be instructed for three years. They are expected to fast. There are now a variety of ministries involved in initiation. Numerous rites such as the imposition of hands, the use of oil, and exorcisms all form part of the initiation picture.

The granting of religious freedom by Constantine in 315 CE resulted in large numbers of converts to Christianity. The intimate and intensive formation previously offered for candidates by the community could no longer be provided. This led to the establishment of more formal structures for initiating converts that still survive in the Lenten season and the revised catechumenate.

During the third and fourth centuries the catechumenate (the formation of new Christians) lasted approximately three years. During that time the catechumens received instructions almost daily and engaged in various ascetical disciplines. The community not only was concerned that the catechumens learn the tradition but was very alert to how well they had begun to put into practice what they had learned.

The best insights into the catechumenate of the third and fourth centuries are found in the writings of the early Church Fathers like Cyril of Jerusalem, John Chrysostom, Theodore of Mopsuestia, and Basil. Their writings include instructions and homilies to the catechumens and the newly baptized that give us some hint of the high expectations placed on them.

The picture which the early Church Fathers give us about the content of the instructions and the community's expectations of candidates is supplemented by Etheria, a pilgrim to the Holy Places, who describes in detail the rites of initiation she witnessed at Jerusalem.[1] While her report is limited to the church at Jerusalem, we can surmise that other similar rites were being practiced elsewhere.

The development of initiation practice presents anything but a uniform picture. As the Christian community spread further east and further west various differences emerged depending to a great extent on the culture of the place.

Besides the development of various rites emerging from cultural adaptations, there were other early developments in initiation practice that significantly contributed to initiation theology and spirituality. One of the most significant influences on initiation theology and spirituality was the increasing practice of infant baptism.

There is already evidence of infant baptism in the *Apostolic Tradition* of Hippolytus and in Tertullian (c. 198 CE). This shifted the weight of baptismal preparedness to the parents and community. Such a change was a contributing factor to the gradual breakdown of the third and fourth century catechumenates. When parents were urged to baptize their infants as soon as possible this began to affect the initiation rites themselves. The rites of initiation formerly regarded as one ritual were now separated. Initiation in the early Church included baptism, a post-baptismal anointing with chrism, and a sharing in the eucharistic table with the community of the faithful. All three ceremonies, presided over by the bishop, constituted in the minds of the people of the time one rite of Christian initiation. In this early period of the Church the three initiation movements would not have been thought of as three separate sacraments, as Catholic theology speaks of them today. But as parents were urged to baptize their infants immediately, they could not always be assured of the bishop's availability. Consequently, parents had their child baptized and even given Communion, but, at least in the West, postponed the anointing with chrism (confirmation) until they could celebrate with the bishop. The concern over the bishop's involvement is an indication of the importance the community placed on his role as chief pastor and celebrant of initiation. His presence was a clear reminder of the candidate's admission into and unity with the universal Church.

With the practice of infant baptism and the separation of the initiation rites there grew a need to explain the three specific movements of initiation and the role of the bishop. The most difficult to explain of these initiation rites is the post-baptismal anointing with chrism and sometimes the imposition of hands. Scholars still question how essential was the anointing with chrism, the number of anointings, and whether this post-baptismal anointing was what at least in Roman Catholic theology is called the sacrament of confirmation. Even today in the baptism of infants and adults, when for some good pastoral reason an individual is not immediately confirmed, there is a post-baptismal anointing with chrism which the Church does not refer to as confirmation. However the gesture is so similar that it raises questions of its precise meaning in the spectrum of initiation rites. The Rite of Christian Initiation of Adults calls for the more traditional sequence of baptism, confirmation, Eucharist to be celebrated in one ritual. It is presumed, in fact, that these three sacraments will be celebrated together even if the bishop is not present to confirm the candidates. The bishop's role in the sacraments of initiation is still maintained in the symbolism of the chrism which must be blessed by him. The bishop's relationship to the candidates is also maintained in a Eucharist celebrated by the bishop with the newly initiated sometime during the year.

The historical sketch of Christian initiation presented here by no means offers a complete history but hopefully suggests the complexity and diversity in the development of initiation practice. In spite of the diversities (which are not necessarily to be taken as opposing or contradictory to each other), we can begin to draw out a number of elements which over the centuries have come to characterize initiation practice and spirituality.

The complex historical features of Christian initiation have most recently converged in the *Rite of Christian Initiation of Adults* proposed by the Roman Catholic Church.[2] In this document we find the elements of a spirituality for Christian initiation that are the product of various ritual and catechetical traditions developed from the beginning of Christianity. While the remainder of this paper will rely upon the Roman Catholic *Rite of Christian Initiation of Adults* as a synthesis or deposit of initiation spirituality, other Christian churches would no doubt be in some accord with the basic themes of spirituality enumerated here.

A. THE ROLE OF THE COMMUNITY

The *Rite of Christian Initiation of Adults* (RCIA) states clearly that "the people of God, represented by the local Church, should always understand and show that the initiation of adults is its concern and the business of all the baptized" (#41).

The connection between convert and community is integral to the very meaning of Christian initiation. Baptism inserts one into the community creating a bond between believer and community as well as between the believer and the Lord. Consequently, the community must make the initiation of new members its concern. Underlying this principle is a firm belief in the importance of the community itself. Christians are not baptized into doctrine or private faith but into a *people.* Christianity owes a great debt to Judaism for its understanding of this *peoplehood.* The First Letter of Peter is an early theological attempt to link the election of Israel to the Christian Church's understanding of itself: "You, however, are a 'chosen race, a royal priesthood, a holy nation, a people he claims for his own to proclaim the glorious works' of the One who called you out of darkness into his marvelous light" (1 Pet 2:9).

For Christians, initiation into the Church is important because salvation comes through the community. The Lord has made a covenant with his people, and it is a covenant that he himself has initiated and sealed with the blood of Christ. In Christian theology this covenant is made between the Lord and his people and is not contracted with separate individuals. Consequently the benefit of the covenant flows from the community.

The RCIA attempts to broaden Christians' appreciation of their bondedness through baptism by concretely expressing the need for the community's involvement in the formation of converts. It becomes quite clear that it is not just the clergy who are responsible for the formation of the convert. The community is expected to expose the converts to its prayer, teaching, morals, and apostolic life. They are to share with the converts their own convictions and way of life. Consequently, what is crucial to the making of new Christians is not what textbooks or classes have been offered but the quality of dialogue between the Christian community and the converts. The exchange between converts and community not only serves the converts but the community as well. They are inspired and challenged to renew their own faith.

One of the striking features of the RCIA is the community's responsibility to judge the readiness of candidates for initiation. In particular, the godparents and those directly involved in the candidates' formation are asked to give public testimony in the Rite of Election regarding the candidates.[3] Christians who view faith as a private affair fail to understand the community's voice in this matter.

The role of the community has remained important in the life of the Church even in the more frequent practice of infant baptism. In the baptism of infants the Church expects the parents to be living examples of the Church's faith. As the child grows and develops in the home, he or she gradually absorbs the life of the Church from the parents and is led to make a conscious commitment of faith. The vocation of the parents to draw their children into the life of the Church is so important that, if parents are not able to make that commitment, the baptism of the child is to be delayed.[4] It is the community's responsibility to offer parents the necessary faith building and catechesis that should precede the child's baptism. What would ordinarily be expected of adult catechumens is expected of the parents, so that to some extent they are drawn into a catechumenal environment which will prepare them to assume their duties as Christian parents.

At various times throughout history the role of the community in initiation became rather minimal. Frequently catechesis prior to adult baptism reverted to the clergy alone. The celebration of baptism for infants and adults was often semi-private, allowing little opportunity for the community to participate in the initiation rites. The role of godparents or sponsors seems to have been the thread to the community's involvement. The godparent or sponsor was expected to be a practicing Catholic, fully initiated through baptism, confirmation and the Eucharist and capable of assuming the responsibility of godparent. While the practical role definition of the godparents or sponsors varied from time to time and place to place, their presence is a consistent testimony to the involvement of the wider community.

If the role of the community appears to be minimal in times past, one reason could be the frequently poor self-understanding of the community. The laity have often felt like second class citizens, unqualified, unholy, and thus unsuited for the care and formation of converts. In the RCIA, however, the Church has proposed not only a renewed picture of initiation, but a renewed sense of what it means to be a member of the Christian community. As the spirit of the RCIA becomes more deeply ingrained in minds and hearts, the Christian community will no doubt grow in self-esteem. In this way the revised rites of Christian initiation will play a significant role in the spirituality of the laity.

B. NEED FOR PERSONAL CONVERSION

The Christian Scriptures offer enough evidence that those who were baptized were also expected to undergo a personal change or conversion in their lives. When Peter and the other apostles were asked "What are we to do, brothers?" Peter answered, "You must reform and be baptized" (Acts

2:38). Jesus himself indicated the cost of being one of his followers when he said, "If a man wishes to come after me, he must deny his very self, take up his cross and begin to follow in my footsteps" (Mt 16:24).[5]

Personal conversion in this context means a free and sincere decision to accept Jesus Christ and to change one's life to conform to his teachings. The need for personal conversion means that preparation for initiation must go beyond catechesis. Although we do not have a great deal of literature available from the early Church that indicates how the process of conversion was fostered, we do find, especially in liturgical texts, an indication of what was expected of candidates for baptism. Theodore of Mopsuestia (fifth century) in his *Instructions to Candidates for Baptism* gives us a hint that more than a knowledge of doctrine was required of candidates.

> He who wishes to draw nigh unto the gift of the holy baptism comes to the church of God. . . . He is received by a duly appointed person—as there is a habit to register those who draw nigh unto baptism—who will question him about his mode of life in order to find out whether it possesses all the requisites of the citizenship of that great city.[6]

What is perhaps one of the strongest witnesses of personal conversion in the history of initiation comes from *The Apostolic Tradition of Hippolytus*. Certain areas of work were simply unacceptable in the third and fourth centuries. Those practicing such professions who wished to be baptized had to change their profession or be refused. Listed as unacceptable we find: actors or pantomimists, charioteers, gladiators, magicians, astrologers, soothsayers, jugglers, military commanders or civic magistrates who wore purple.[7]

At certain points in history the expectations of conversion associated with baptism have tended to become more legalistic. This is especially true during those times when the Church was faced with either large numbers of lapsed members or when the number of converts became so large that the community could not offer direct moral guidance. At those times laws had to be enacted simply to maintain minimum expectations for membership.[8]

In the RCIA, expectations of personal conversion prior to baptism are attested to ritually in the questions addressed to the godparents in the Rite of Election, at which catechumens are formally chosen or elected for the initiation sacraments at Easter. The presider asks the godparents, "Have they been true to the word they have received and begun to walk in God's presence?" (#144).

With the practice of infant baptism, we obviously could not expect the infants to undergo a personal conversion prior to baptism. However, there has always been the expectation that the parents would provide a home environment where the child's faith could mature and reach a personal conversion.[9]

It should be noted that for Roman Catholics the conversion experience is never a sudden, complete act but rather an ongoing experience. Consequently, even though one may have reached a particular turning point in one's life, the conversion is really never complete in that one's life is constantly turning toward the Lord. It is with that understanding that Lent has become a season of conversion for converts and for seasoned Christians. For the six weeks prior to Easter, Christians accompany catechumens on their journey toward baptism, retracing their own initiation through the liturgy and discipline of the Lenten season.

> Lent is a memorial or a preparation for baptism and a time of penance. It renews the community of the faithful together with the catechumens and makes them ready to celebrate the paschal mystery which the sacraments of initiation apply to each individual" (#21).

C. IDENTIFICATION WITH CHRIST'S DEATH AND RESURRECTION

One of the most consistent themes of initiation spirituality through the years has been the identification of the baptized with the person of Jesus Christ and the conception of the baptismal ritual as an imitation of the dying and rising of Christ. St. Paul spoke of the experience of initiation as an identification with Christ. In his Letter to the Galatians he wrote, "For all of you who have been baptized into union with Christ have clothed yourselves with Christ" (Gal 3:27). "It is no longer I that live, but Christ that lives in me" (Gal 2:20). St. Paul saw the baptismal plunge as an imitation of Christ's dying and rising by which the fruit of that sacred event is directly applied to the candidate.

> Are you not aware that we who were baptized into Christ Jesus were baptized into his death? Through baptism into his death we were buried with him, so that, just as Christ was raised from the dead by the glory of the Father, we too might live a new life" (Rom 6:3–4).

The Fathers, especially in the East, seemed to pursue Paul's initial theological interpretation of the baptismal act. In his *Mystagogic Catecheses,* Cyril of Jerusalem (c. 350 CE) explores Paul's imagery of imitating Christ's death and resurrection:

> What a wonder and what a paradox! We have not actually died, we have not really been buried, and we have not, in reality, after having been crucified, risen again. But the imitation is effected in an image, salvation in reality. Christ was really crucified, really placed in a tomb; he really rose again. And all these things were done through love for us, so that, sharing by imitation in his sufferings, we might truly obtain salvation.[10]

It is not difficult to see how Paul and Cyril of Jerusalem saw the baptismal ceremony as imitating Christ's death and resurrection. The baptismal fonts of the early Church were much larger and deeper than the fonts used today. Some of the fonts or baptismal pools resembled a tomb. To witness a catechumen going down into the tomb-like font conjured images of death, just as rising from the water resembled a resurrection. Even though the baptismal fonts shrank in later years, the symbolism found in Paul and Cyril of Jerusalem continued.

In our own day, the Church has encouraged more substantial fonts so that the baptism of infants at least can be celebrated by immersion.[11]

Sharing Christ's Priestly Vocation

The Christian's identification with Christ through baptism has greatly affected Christian spirituality, as it finds expression in an understanding of the *priesthood of the laity.* Christians view Christ as Priest, one who offers to God the Father the perfect sacrifice in which he is the victim and the priest. Because of the Christian's close identification with Christ, he or she shares in the priesthood of Jesus.

During the Reformation, Christian churches held opposing views on what it meant to share in the priesthood of Jesus Christ. The reformers held that there was no specific order of priesthood except that which was granted to all Christians through baptism. And since they rejected the notion of the Eucharist as sacrifice, they saw no need for a cultic priesthood in the Church.[12]

The Council of Trent (1563 CE) reacted to the reformers and maintained the Roman Catholic position that there was indeed a distinct order of priesthood.[13] This led to an avoidance of "priesthood of the faithful," for fear of siding with the reformers. The Roman Church gradually became more comfortable with acknowledging the laity's sharing in Christ's vocation as priest. But concessions to this spirituality were made very carefully. In his encyclical *Mediator Dei* (1947 CE), Pope Pius XII said:

> The fact that the faithful take part in the Eucharistic Sacrifice does not mean that they also possess the power of the priesthood. . . . The rites and prayers of the Mass show no less clearly that the offering of the Victim is made by the priest together with the people. . . . And there is no wonder that the faithful are accorded this privilege: by reason of their baptism Christians are in the Mystical Body and become by a common title members of Christ the Priest; by the character that is grown upon their souls they are appointed to the worship of God, and therefore, according to their condition, they share in the priesthood of Christ himself.[14]

In the *Dogmatic Constitution on the Church,* the fathers of the Second Vatican Council reaffirmed belief in the priesthood of the laity, while at the same time clarifying more precisely the distinction between an ordained order of priesthood and the priesthood that the laity enjoy through baptism.

> Though they differ essentially and not only in degree, the common priesthood of the faithful and the ministerial or hierarchical priesthood are nonetheless ordered one to another; each in its own proper way shares in the one priesthood of Christ. The ministerial priest, by the sacred power that he has, forms and rules the priestly people; in the person of Christ he effects the eucharistic sacrifice and offers it to God in the name of all the people. The faithful indeed, by virtue of their royal priesthood, participate in the offering of the Eucharist. They exercise that priesthood, too, by the reception of the sacraments, prayer and thanksgiving, the witness of a holy life, abnegation and active charity.[15]

While the use of the term "priesthood of the faithful" may have fluctuated from time to time, its underlying reality has been the basis in Christian piety for the Christian's participation in *worship* and a call to *witness.*

Worship

As one can deduce from the preceding quotations, Christians cannot view themselves as mere spectators of worship. While there is a hierarchy of ministries, the ministry of the assembly is by no means insignificant.

The Christian assembly together with the ordained priest offers one sacrifice of praise and thanksgiving. The liturgical renewal, especially evident in the Roman Catholic community since the Second Vatican Council, is tied very closely to a renewed appreciation of the faithful's identification with Christ the Priest, through whom and in whose name the assembly offers its worship.

In the RCIA, the right and privilege of the baptized to celebrate the Eucharist is brought out clearly when, after the liturgy of the word, the catechumens are dismissed; they are not yet joined to Christ the Priest through baptism and thus are not able to offer the sacrifice of Christ. It is also significant that the RCIA calls for formation in the liturgical prayer of the Church. In other words, the catechumen must learn how to pray the liturgy of the Church, since this is the Christian's vocation.

In those times when the "priesthood of the faithful" was played down, Christians tended to become mere spectators at worship. The ordained ministers gradually usurped many of the roles previously enjoyed by the assembly, subtly conveying to the faithful that it was only the ordained priest who offered worship. This in turn led to a deterioration of the laity's self-concept, so that they perceived themselves as unholy and unfit to actively participate in the rites of the Church.

As the ordained ministry was more and more accentuated, there also developed a sharp division between laity and clergy, which only gave further impetus to clericalism.

Recent liturgical renewal has above all attempted to reinstate the Christian in his or her dignity, as one who shares in the priesthood of the faithful and thus has the right and obligation to engage in worship. Resistance on the part of many to liturgical change, especially the involvement of the laity in liturgical roles, may well be due to a lost appreciation of what it means to be one with Christ the Priest.

Witness

As the Christian is so intimately identified with Christ through baptism, the mission of Christ becomes the vocation of the Christian. Jesus described his mission when he said, "I must announce the good news of the reign of God." Jesus accomplished that mission by revealing God's Kingdom through his words and deeds, signs and miracles, and most especially by his death and resurrection.

Peter described the Christian's participation in Jesus' mission by calling the baptized "a people he (God) claims for his own to proclaim the glorious works of the One who called you out of darkness into his marvelous light" (1 Pet 2:9).

The early Church saw that participation in Christ's mission symbolized in a special way in the post-baptismal sealing with chrism or myron. Cyril of Jerusalem conceived of the anointing of the newly baptized as an imitation of the Spirit that descended upon Jesus when he rose from the waters after being baptized by John. "In the same manner for you also, after you had come up from the pool of sacred streams there was the chrismation, the exact figure of that with which Christ was christened; and this was the Holy Spirit."[16] As Christ assumed his mission after being anointed with the Spirit, so the Christian, according to Cyril of Jerusalem, shares in the mission of Jesus once he or she is anointed with chrism. For in the anointing the Spirit is given for Christian service.

> According to Cyril the anointing bespeaks a particular communication of the Holy Spirit, and by his typology of Christ's baptism in the Jordan he shows that this communication of the Holy Spirit transforms the Christian according to a particular modality of the life of Christ, namely the modality of Christ's Messianic mission.[17]

Catholic Christians continue to recognize in the post-baptismal anointing with chrism or confirmation that same identification with Christ and his mission that Cyril spoke of long ago. In the address to candidates in the current ritual for confirmation, baptism, confirmation and the call to witness are brought together:

> Born again in baptism, you have become members of Christ and of his priestly people. Now you are to share in the outpouring of the Holy Spirit among us, the Spirit sent by the Lord upon the apostles at Pentecost and given by them and their successors to the baptized.
>
> The promised strength of the Holy Spirit which you are to receive, will make you more like Christ, and help you to be witnesses to his suffering, death, and resurrection. It will strengthen you to be active members of the Church and to build up the Body of Christ in faith and love.[18]

A prayer for the gifts of wisdom, understanding, right judgment and courage, knowledge and reverence and the spirit of wonder and awe in God's presence is then offered so that the newly anointed will be strengthened to carry out the mission of Jesus.

The most contemporary teaching on the responsibility of each Christian to share in the mission of Jesus is outlined in Pope Paul VI's Apostolic Exhortation, *Evangelization in the Modern World.* In this document Pope Paul VI describes Jesus as the first evangelizer, the one who announces the Father's Kingdom. But he goes on to say that it is the whole Church that takes up that vocation of Jesus.

> Having been born consequently out of being sent, the Church in her turn is sent by Jesus. The Church remains in the world when the Lord of glory returns to the Father. . . . It is above all his mission and his condition of being an evangelizer that she is called upon to continue. For the Christian community is never closed in upon itself. The intimate life of this community—the life of listening to the Word and the Apostles' teaching, charity lived in a fraternal way, the sharing of bread—this intimate life only acquires its full meaning when it becomes a witness, when it evokes admiration and conversion, and when it becomes the preaching and proclamation of the Good News. Thus it is the whole Church that receives the mission to evangelize, and the work of each individual member is important for the whole.[19]

While all Christians participate in the mission of Jesus, each member of the Church exercises that responsibility in a different way. Out of the one mission of the Church various ministries emerge. Every Christian is called to ministry in the wide sense as an empowerment to serve others, but not every Christian is called to ministry in a formal sense such as in the ordained ministry whereby the Church formally chooses an individual for the exercise of a particular office.[20] Once again this relates to the concept of the "priesthood of the faithful," which as we have already seen calls for careful distinctions in a differentiation of roles among the baptized.

Because the sharing of Jesus' mission is so essential to what it means to be a Christian, the RCIA calls upon the local community to provide an apostolic orientation in the catechumenate process.

> Since the Church's life is apostolic, catechumens should also learn how to work actively with others to spread the Gospel and build up the Church by the testimony of their lives and the profession of their faith.[21]

As the community assumes responsibility for forming converts in an apostolic spirit, it will be challenged to evaluate its own witness.

D. LENT/EASTER: THE SEASON FOR INITIATION

Any discussion of Christian Initiation and its effect on Christian spirituality must also include the seasons of Lent/Easter. These seasons carry the Church's spirituality of initiation into the mainstream of Christian life by placing the rites of initiation into the Christian calendar. The RCIA states: "The rite of initiation is normally arranged so that the sacraments will be celebrated during the Easter Vigil,"[22] and it ties initiation to the Lent and Easter seasons:

> The whole initiation has a paschal character, since the initiation of Christians is the first sacramental sharing in the death and rising of Christ and since, moreover, the time of purification and enlightenment or illumination ordinarily takes place during Lent, with the post-baptismal catechesis or mystagogia during the Easter season. In this way Lent achieves its full force as a profound preparation of the elect, and the Easter Vigil is considered the proper time for the sacraments of initiation.[23]

As the Church celebrates the dying and rising of Christ at the Easter Vigil, it becomes most appropriate to baptize candidates on the same night since they will die and rise with Christ in the waters of baptism. Thus, through baptism, Christians make the Easter or Paschal Mystery their own.

The appropriateness of Easter for baptism was attested to as early as the fourth century. The Fathers frequently referred to Easter as the proper time for initiation. The testimony of Basil the Great (fourth century) is characteristic of the Fathers' views.

> Therefore any time is suitable for obtaining salvation through baptism, be it day or night, or at a precise hour or the briefest moment. But assuredly that time should be considered most appropriate which is closest in spirit to it. What could be more akin to baptism than the day of the Pasch? For that day commemorates the Resurrection, and baptism makes the resurrection possible for us. Let us receive the grace of the resurrection on the day of the Resurrection.[24]

St. Leo the Great (fifth century) later felt it necessary to admonish those who were choosing other feasts of the calendar for baptism. In a letter to all the bishops throughout Sicily, Leo was intent on establishing

Easter as the primary date for baptism, with Pentecost as an acceptable option when pastorally necessary. The following excerpt from his pastoral letter makes it quite clear that he regards the Easter date as a derivative of apostolic practice.

> Accordingly, when it reached my ears on reliable testimony that in what is one of the chief sacraments of the Church you depart from the practice of the Apostles' constitution by administering the sacrament of baptism to greater numbers on the feast of Epiphany than at Eastertide, I was surprised that you or your predecessors could have introduced so unreasonable an innovation as to confound the mysteries of the two festivals and believe there was no difference between the day on which Christ was worshiped by the wise men and that on which he rose again from the dead.[25]

It should be added to Pope Leo's credit that in the same letter he did allow for baptism at any time when there was danger of death.

In light of the writings of Basil and Leo, the simple rubric given in the RCIA for the preference of Easter for initiation appears very light. The wedding of baptism and Easter, however, does not simply stand on statements that baptism should take place at the Easter Vigil. The whole forty days of Lent that precede the Easter Vigil and the fifty days of Easter time that follow surround the Vigil in such a way that it is the climax of Lent and Easter. During Lent the Church prepares for baptism and during the Easter season reflects upon the implications of baptismal initiation. During Lent the Church not only prepares candidates for baptism, but prepares the faithful for baptismal renewal at Easter. Christians are encouraged to fast, do penance, engage in intensive prayer and perform works of charity to purify themselves and in a sense retrace the steps of their own conversion and initiation. The catechumens become a challenging sign to the whole community to renew their own commitment to the Lord and the Church.

The community is expected to engage in the discipline of Lent for the sake of the catechumens so that they may undergo a true conversion of mind and heart. The community's Lenten discipline then is not a private ascetical practice, but an activity of the Church for the good of the Church. The catechumens in turn are not simply expected to adopt an individual form of asceticism and mortification in preparation for baptism, but to become part of an activity of the Church as a whole.

The prayers and Scriptures of the Lent and Easter seasons are so strongly initiatory in tone that to initiate adults outside the Easter Vigil weakens the rites of initiation as well as the liturgy of Lent and Easter. The references to initiation in the official liturgical prayers of the Church are another indication of the involvement of the community in the initiation process. The community is not only exposed to prayers for the candidates, but in these prayers identifies with them. The Opening Prayer of the Mass for the Saturday of the Fifth Week of Lent is an example of this.

God our Father,
you always work to save us,
and now we rejoice in the great love
you give to your chosen people.
Protect all who are about to become your children
and continue to bless those who are already baptized.

The Lenten liturgical texts place a great emphasis on repentance and conversion and apply them to both the catechumens and the faithful. The Easter texts emphasize the baptism of the new Christians as well as the baptismal renewal of the faithful.

Father,
you give your Church constant growth
by adding new members to your family.
Help us to put into action in our lives
the baptism we have received with faith.
(Opening Prayer for Monday in the Octave of Easter)

God of mercy,
you wash away our sins in water,
you give us new birth in the Spirit,
and redeem us in the blood of Christ.
As we celebrate Christ's resurrection
increase our awareness of these blessings,
and renew your gift of life within us.
(Opening Prayer for the Second Sunday of Easter)

The Scripture selections for the Lenten season, especially in the first year of the three year cycle of biblical readings, are particularly appropriate for the initiation of adults. These traditional Gospel stories serve as instructions for the catechumens. The story of the woman at the well (Jn 4:5–42) teaches the catechumens to thirst for living water. The account of the man born blind (Jn 9:1–41) calls the catechumens out of the dark to follow the light, who is the Lord. And the story of Lazarus being brought back to life (Jn 11:1–45) powerfully draws the catechumens to the Lord who has power over life and death and stirs the catechumens to ponder the meaning of life and death and the promise of eternal life. Delivering these instructions within the context of the community's worship is a clear indication of the community's involvement in the whole initiation process. As this instruction takes place in the midst of the community the assembly obviously profits from the same process, making a parallel journey of faith with the catechumens.

E. SACRAMENTAL TYPOLOGY

Of all the factors that have contributed to Christian initiation spirituality none have probably been more pronounced than sacramental typology. Sacramental typology looks to the Hebrew Scriptures and in particular to the great events of salvation history and views these sacred events as types or figures of Christian baptism. The purpose of looking back to the great salvation events is not to interpret them as a hidden form of Christian baptism as if their meaning and significance could only be validated in the Christian era. On the contrary, sacramental typology first of all recalls the great events of God's action in history and respects these events in their own context. Secondly, sacramental typology sees God's continuing action now in the present form of the sacraments as a prolongation of the great works of God.

Sacramental typology flows directly from the Scriptures and so forms a biblical theology of initiation. Because the biblical images are so strong, sacramental typology has been able to successfully influence the piety of ordinary Christians. Modern liturgical texts continue to employ a sacramental typology in new liturgical compositions.[26] Religious art, past and present, also gives witness to the persistent appeal of sacramental typology especially witnessed in the decoration of baptistries.

The origins of sacramental typology are already evident in the Christian Scriptures. In the First Letter of Peter we find the great deluge used as a figure of baptism. "At that time, a few persons, eight in all, escaped in the ark through the water. You are now saved by a baptismal bath which corresponds to this exactly" (1 Pet 3:18–21). In the First Letter to the

Corinthians, Paul sees a baptismal motif in the Red Sea experience: "Brothers, I want you to remember this: our fathers were all under the cloud and all passed through the sea; by the cloud and the sea all of them were baptized into Moses" (1 Cor 10:1–5). In John's Gospel we find an early theological interpretation of the Eucharist that recalls the manna given the Israelites in the desert: "I solemnly assure you, it was not Moses who gave you bread from the heavens; it is my Father who gives you the real heavenly bread" (Jn 6:32). "Your ancestors ate manna in the desert, but they died. This is the bread that comes down from heaven for a man to eat and never die" (Jn 6:49–50).

Tertullian (third century) would probably receive credit for being the first of the Fathers to draw a full array of baptismal types from the Hebrew Scriptures in the earliest theological work on baptism, *De Baptismo.* But Tertullian was by no means the only one of the Fathers or spiritual writers to develop a sacramental typology. While there are various lists of types found in the Hebrew Scriptures, there are a number which have become more commonly used.

1. The Primitive Waters of Genesis

The primordial waters brought forth life and the Spirit of God hovered over the waters. Baptism is a new creation. The baptismal waters are embued with the presence and power of the Spirit and bring forth new life in the baptized.[27]

2. The Deluge

We have already seen how Peter made use of the deluge to speak of the destructive power of water. This destructive characteristic of water relates to a spirituality of baptism as a configuration of Christ's death and resurrection.

As sinful humanity in Noah's time was destroyed by a judgment of God in the flood, and Noah, the just man, was saved to be the first born of a new human race, so in baptism the old man is destroyed by means of the sacrament of water and the person who emerges from the baptismal font belongs to a new creation.

The ark too finds a place in Christian spirituality, becoming a symbol of the Church that houses the saved.

3. The Exodus

The biblical event most frequently used in sacramental typology is that of the Exodus. As Jean Daniélou points out:

> At the beginning of the Christian era, the initiation of proselytes into the Jewish community included, besides circumcision, a baptism. . . . The purpose of this initiation was to cause the proselyte to go through the sacrament received by the people at the time of the crossing of the Red Sea. The baptism of the proselytes was, then, a kind of imitation of the Exodus. This is important in showing us that the link between Baptism and the crossing of the Red Sea existed already in Judaism and that therefore it gives us the true symbolism of Baptism, as being not primarily a purification, but a deliverance and a creation.[28]

The Fathers were fond of using the Exodus to unfold the richness of God's saving activity in baptism. Basil's reflection is characteristic of a patristic commentary:

> What concerns the Exodus of Israel is told us in order to signify those who are saved by Baptism. . . . The sea is the figure of Baptism, since it delivered the people from Pharaoh, as Baptism from the tyranny of the devil. The sea killed the enemy; so in Baptism, our enmity to God is destroyed. The people came out of the sea whole and safe; we also come out of the water as living men from among the dead.[29]

The account of Exodus is still a required Scripture passage at the Church's Easter Vigil, affirming its place in Christian initiation spirituality.

4. The Pasch

Christian writers from the beginning of the Church's life have looked to the Passover to understand the depth of the Easter Mystery. It is one of the chief figures in sacramental typology. The celebration of Easter and the initiation rites have been placed in the framework of the Jewish Pasch, and so its proximity to Passover has led to a development of several spiritual parallels. The Passover recalls the deliverance from Egypt and the passing over of the angel of death. The Christian sees baptism and Easter as a deliverance from slavery and sin and passing over from death to new life. The blood of the passover lamb that marked the doorposts of the

Israelites is for Christians the blood of Christ that preserves them from eternal death and seals their covenant with God. In Christian spirituality Christ becomes the lamb slain and eaten. This Passover food, the Christian Eucharist, parallels the Passover Supper and stands as a link between the Passover Meal and the Messianic Banquet.

There are other sacramental typologies that have been used throughout history: Joshua crossing the Jordan, Moses striking the rock that gives water, manna in the desert, Psalm 23 (the good shepherd) and Psalm 42 (deer running to streams). These are but a few of the many biblical events used in sacramental typology. What should be made clear, however, is that sacramental typology does not intend to discredit the original saving acts of God preserved in the ancient Scriptures. As already mentioned, Christian sacramental typology reaffirms God's saving activity in the past and sees his activity continued in the present celebration of the sacraments. The use of these biblical figures has enabled Christians to see God's presence more clearly in the celebration of the Christian sacraments.

CONCLUSION

The Rites of Christian Initiation have long influenced the spirituality of Christians. Not only the ritual texts themselves but the ritual actions and the sacred seasons during which they are celebrated have prompted theological and spiritual reflections that have translated into the piety of ordinary Christians. The more involved the Christian community has been in the process and celebration of initiation, the closer it has been to the root of the Christian creed that proclaims Christ crucified and risen. With the promulgation of the *Rite of Christian Initiation of Adults* the Christian community is called to a renewed involvement in the making of new Christians. This will hopefully take Christians back to the source of Christian spirituality, the Paschal Mystery.

Sacramental typology has offered Christians a biblical spirituality of Christian initiation. It continues to be a valuable, sound component of Christian spirituality. However, if Christians are to take full advantage of a sacramental typology rooted in the Hebrew Scriptures, they will need to become more familiar with and appreciative of the biblical experiences of Israel. Not to be so informed could lead to a disregard or misreading of the past which is not really past at all, but a testimony of God's timeless gift of his presence.

NOTES

1. *The Pilgrimage of Etheria,* M.L. McLure, C.L. Feltoe, eds. (New York: Macmillan, 1963).

2. *Rite of Christian Initiation of Adults* (Washington, D.C.: United States Catholic Conference, 1974).

3. *Ibid.,* #144.

4. *Instruction on Infant Baptism* (Vatican City: Congregation for the Doctrine of the Faith, 1980), cf. para. 30.

5. Cf. also Acts 2:41; 18:8; Mk 16:16.

6. Theodore of Mopsuestia, "Instructions to Candidates for Baptism," II, Sermon 2, in E.C. Whitaker, ed., *Documents of the Baptismal Liturgy* (London: SPCK, 1970).

7. *The Apostolic Tradition of Hippolytus,* #16, in edition translated by Burton Scott Easton (Cambridge: Cambridge Univ. Press, 1962), p. 42.

8. Daniel B. Stevick, "Types of Baptismal Spirituality," in *Worship* 47, No. 1 (January 1973).

9. Cf. *Instruction on Infant Baptism,* para. 15, 30–33.

10. Cf. Jean Daniélou, *The Bible and the Liturgy* (Notre Dame: Univ. of Notre Dame, 1956), p. 44.

11. *Environment and Art in Catholic Worship* (Washington, D.C.: United States Catholic Conference, 1978), #76–77. Cf. also General Introduction to Christian Initiation, #22, found in the *Rite of Baptism for Children* (Washington, D.C.: United States Catholic Conference, 1970).

12. Cf. Richard P. McBrien, *Catholicism* (Minneapolis: Winston Press, 1980), p. 805. Also, *Ministries in the Church,* Study Text 3 (Washington, D.C.: United States Catholic Conference, 1974), pp. 17–21.

13. Josef Neuner, Heinrich Roos, *The Teachings of the Catholic Church,* Karl Rahner, ed. (New York: Alba House, 1966), pp. 342–346.

14. *Ibid.,* pp. 347–349.

15. Austin P. Flannery, ed., *Documents of Vatican II* (Grand Rapids: Eerdmans, 1975), "Dogmatic Constitution on the Church," #10, p. 361.

16. Cyril of Jerusalem, *Mystagogic Catecheses,* III.

17. Hugh M. Riley, *Christian Initiation* (Washington, D.C.: Catholic University Press, 1974), p. 369.

18. *Rite of Christian Initiation of Adults,* #229.

19. Pope Paul VI, *On Evangelization in the Modern World* (Washington, D.C.: United States Catholic Conference, 1975), #13.

20. Richard P. McBrien, *op. cit.,* pp. 842–846.

21. *Rite of Christian Initiation of Adults,* #19.1.

22. *Ibid.,* #58.

23. *Ibid.,* #8.

24. Basil the Great "Protreptic on Holy Baptism," #1, in André Hamman,

ed. *Baptism, Ancient Liturgies and Patristic Texts* (New York: Alba House, 1967), p. 76.

25. *Ibid.,* pp. 230–233.

26. The Prayer for the Blessing of Baptismal Water is a perfect example of this; cf. *Rite of Christian Initiation of Adults,* #215.

27. Cf. Tertullian, *De Baptismo,* para. 2, 3, 4.

28. Jean Daniélou, *op. cit.,* pp. 88–89.

29. *Ibid.,* p. 90.

7. Christian Influences on Jewish Customs

Joseph Gutmann

Judah ben Samuel (called *he-Hasid,* the Pietist) sadly observed that "Jewish customs (*minhagim*) in many places [of Germany] are like those practiced by non-Jews [i.e., Christians]."[1] Judah the *Hasid's* statement represents no minor irony when viewed in the light of his own teachings. His early life was spent in the Rhenish cities of Worms and Speyer and in his latter years he resided in Regensburg, where he died in 1217. The *Sefer Hasidim,* the best source for studying his teachings, reveals the influence of feudal German Christianity, especially as practiced in the mendicant and monastic orders. Judah emerges from these pages, which read like a collection of *exempla,* as the spokesman of the *hasidei-ashkenaz*—an elite group of German-Jewish Pietists who translated suffering, asceticism, penitence and even poverty into religious virtues held to be of benefit in the world to come. Judah the *Hasid,* like the saintly monks, led by example; he was the paragon of pietistic values for his Jewish disciples. His work, filled with miracles, popular magic and superstitions, much like those of contemporary Christians, stressed an other-worldly salvation attainable by love, piety, penitence, confession and atonement.[2]

The encounter of Judaism with medieval feudal Christianity, so vividly documented in the *Sefer Hasidim,* was a recent development. Jews entered the Franco-German lands during the ninth century as itinerant international merchants providing the rulers of Western Christendom with much coveted luxury goods from the East. During the tenth and eleventh centuries, they began settling in such Rhenish cities as Worms, Speyer and Mainz; as sedentary merchants there, they played an important role aiding and stimulating the growth of burgeoning feudal cities. By the twelfth century they were heavily involved as large-scale money-lenders in vast Christian building projects. Emperors, nobles and clergymen alike during this period vied with one another to offer Jews significant privileges. The Jews, their lives and property protected by charters, were moderately taxed and granted considerable autonomy; their communities in Germany flourished. By the thirteenth century, however, the crown, the nobility and the Church, all heavily indebted to Jewish financiers, sought to escape repayment by subjecting Jews to a campaign of ideological vilification. Jews were accused of and tried for host desecration, deicide, and the ritual murder of Christian children. Their once favorable status progressively deteriorated in the declining medieval German feudal structure. Reduced to a servile or even pariah legal status, they were now constantly plagued by confiscatory taxation and by expulsion and became mere pawns of their feudal rulers, who saw fit to buy, sell or barter the humiliated, largely impoverished, Jews at will.[3] It is against this backdrop that Ashkenazi Judaism (originally only Franco-German Jewry was embraced by this designation) emerged, locked into autonomous Jewish communities within the decentralized German feudal system. This new Judaism, which took shape between the twelfth and fifteenth centuries, clearly refracted and bore the imprint of the Christian feudal world.

The intention of this study is to examine the emergence of unique and novel Jewish customs centering around the Jewish life cycle—some of them still practiced today—customs which indisputably reflect the Jewish involvement with medieval German Christianity. While early Christianity's indebtedness to Judaism has frequently been studied and is well-known, the influence that medieval Catholicism exerted on Ashkenazi Judaism in its formative stages has generally been overlooked. The reasons for this gap are probably twofold. First, it is attributable to an inadequate Jewish historiography which insisted on submerging the rich diversity of the Jewish historical experience by imposing an undifferentiated unity linking together Jews of all periods.[4] Second, many centuries of hostility, degradation and persecution at Christian hands made Jews reluctant to examine, let alone acknowledge, the fact that many rites of Ashkenazi Judaism may have been inspired by Christianity—the avowed enemy. Thus, such Jewish scholars as Jacob Lauterbach and Solomon Freehof have authoritatively explored the Jewish sources describing the development of some novel Ashkenazi customs, but generally have avoided tracing or investigating comparable Christian customs that may have given rise to Jewish practices. Similarly, nineteenth-century Jewish scholars like Moritz Güdemann and Leopold Löw contented themselves with discreet footnotes hinting at Christian influence.[5]

> [Yet] the history of the Jews [and their religious practices] is a history of involvement. It cannot be separated from the larger context of which it is a part. It is by its very nature simultaneously a history of an entity linked lineally through time and a history of diverse civilizations, cultures and societies. It is the history of the Ancient Near East, the Hellenistic and Roman worlds, the Sasanian Empire, the Moslem and Christian epochs. Wherever we turn in Jewish history we are confronted with involvement—an involvement so interwoven with the texture of the total pattern that to abstract the so-called Jewish element is to do violence not only to Jewish history but to the history of the larger complex as well.[6]

Jewish involvement with Catholic German society roughly between the twelfth and fifteenth centuries, as seen in its life cycle ceremonies, reveals a distinct pattern that inextricably testifies to the complex interrelationship of Ashkenazi Jews with their medieval German Christian neighbors. Jews shared not only Christian fears and anxieties, but also Christian folk life, superstitions, and customs which were ingeniously adapted and transformed for Jewish use.

Although circumcision is one of the oldest and most sacred Jewish rites—marking the entry of the male child into the covenant of Abraham on the eighth day after his birth—several customs introduced by medieval German Jews were originally connected with the sacrament of Baptism. The shifting of the Jewish ceremony from the home to the synagogue during the Gaonic (post-Talmudic) period helped expedite this process. From the time the Jewish child was born until the circumcision ceremony, it was deemed necessary in medieval Germany to safeguard the child against demons, especially the female demon Lilith,[7] to whom popular belief attributed an eagerness to harm the mother and the child. To ward off her evil influence, talismans and amulets were hung on the child and placed around a room of the woman in childbed.[8] Anxiety was at its height on the eve of the circumcision day. This night was considered the most dangerous time of all, since it was believed that demons and evil spirits would make a final concerted effort to injure mother and child. To protect both mother and child, a night vigil was instituted in the Middle Ages.

This medieval Jewish vigil was popularly known as *Wachnacht* (night watch). Relatives and friends gathered in the home to study (*lernen*) and recite prayers during the night so that the child would not be bewitched (*benommen*) or hurt; popular belief held that *brit milah* (the covenant of circumcision) ended the power of all evil spirits and demons. A related ceremony was employed by German Christians the night before Baptism, as they too believed that the power of evil spirits and demons held over mother and child was broken only with Baptism.[9]

Three days prior to circumcision it was customary, especially in the Rhineland, to call out in the streets "Zu der Judsch Kerz" (= *Jüdisch-Kerz,* to the circumcision candle) in order to summon Jewish women to the house of the woman in childbed. Assembled there, they would usually prepare twelve small candles and one large candle, all to be lit in the synagogue during the circumcision ceremony. The twelve small candles symbolized the twelve tribes of Israel; the large candle was called *ner tamid* (eternal light). Among Christians, it was also customary to light twelve small candles and one large candle—in connection with Baptism. Here, of course, the twelve symbolized the twelve apostles and the large one stood for Jesus.[10] Similarly, the child was brought into the synagogue through a special door, known as *Judsch Tirchen* (= *Jüdisch-Tür,* circumcision door)—while a special church door was also employed for the Christian sacrament of Baptism.[11]

On the afternoon of the fourth Sabbath after the birth of a child, a ceremony was held in the Jewish home. This ceremony usually followed the synagogal Sabbath morning services, which the mother had attended for the first time since her confinement. The purpose of the gathering was to give the child a secular or civil name—a Hebrew name had already been bestowed on the boy at the circumcision ceremony. Known as the *Hollekreisch* (also *Holegrasch* or *shem ha'arisah* = cradle name) ceremony, it was first mentioned in the fourteenth century and was apparently restricted mainly to southern Germany, where it was still practiced in some Jewish communities in the twentieth century. The children encircled the cradle—boys in the case of a male child and girls in case of a female birth—and lifted the cradle three times (in some communities the *hazzan,* the cantor, lifted the cradle) while they called out a formula beginning with "Hollekreisch, Hollekreisch, what shall we name the child?" The name *Hollekreisch* has been variously explained as stemming from Hebrew (*hol kara,* i.e., scream or cry out the non-Hebrew name, or profane naming), from French (*haler* or *haut la crèche* = lift up or raise the cradle), or related to *Frau Holle* (or Hulda, Holda), a witch who attacks infants. *Hollekreisch,* in the latter case, simply means either to encircle (*kreisen*) or call off (*kreischen*) Dame Holle before she injures the child.[12]

This curious ceremony was undoubtedly borrowed by Jews from their Christian south German neighbors. Vestiges of such ceremonies are found in folk-ditties stemming from that region.[13]

One of the most important ceremonies celebrated today in the Jewish life cycle is the *Bar-Mitzvah* (son of the commandment or religious duty), yet no trace of this ceremony can be found in Jewish sources before the thirteenth century and it appears to have been widely practiced in the Rhineland by the fourteenth century. Usually on the first Sabbath after his thirteenth birthday, the boy was called up to the Torah (Pentateuch) for the first time and read from the Torah Scroll to indicate that he had now reached the age of legal and religious majority, could be admitted to membership in the synagogue, and could be counted as a responsible member of the Jewish community. He was now liable for the observance of all the commandments, and to symbolize this transition, at the time the son was called to the Torah, the father recited the following formula: "Blessed be He who has divested me of responsibility for this one."[14] It is interesting to note that this ceremony was probably inspired by the Christian Confirmation rite. Originally Confirmation was performed at or shortly after Baptism, but by the thirteenth century it was deferred to the year of discretion variously interpreted as ten, twelve, or fourteen. Called now the *sacrament of adolescence* or *spiritual progress* (Baptism is considered spiritual birth), it confirmed or renewed the baptismal vows of grace. Confirmation marked the recipient's mature acceptance of faith and his admittance to full privileges in the Church as he took upon himself now the obligations of confession and Communion.[15]

During the Talmudic period, the Jewish wedding consisted of two distinct ceremonies. In the betrothal ceremony known as *erusin* (or *kiddushin*), the woman was legally married, although she remained in her father's house. Usually the nuptial ceremony (*nissuin*) was held one year later. By the Middle Ages, these two ceremonies became combined in German Jewish communities and often took place on the same day.[16] Somewhat earlier the Christian betrothal and nuptial ceremonies, which also had been held separately, were combined by the Church, and it was this Christian practice which probably influenced the Jewish practice.[17]

Again, the original betrothal ceremony was superseded by new Jewish engagement ceremonies, and these, too, were probably patterned after similar practices of their Christian neighbors. In Germany, the custom of a *Knas-Mahl* (penalty feast) arose in the late Middle Ages. This was essentially an engagement party held after the conditions (*tenaim*) of the forthcoming match were written out by both parties in a formal contract and a monetary fine (*knas*) was stipulated in case one of the parties wanted to break the engagement at a later time.[18]

A preliminary German Jewish wedding ceremony, first recorded by Jacob ha-Levi Möllin (ca. 1355–1427) of Mainz-Worms, was called *Spinnholz.*[19] On the Sabbath preceding the wedding, a series of festivities—feasting, dancing, singing and merrymaking—took place and the bridegroom was especially honored at synagogue services.[20] The origin of this ceremony is obscure. It has been linked to the distaff of the spinner the bride received as part of her trousseau, a symbol of feminine domesticity, from *spinalzare* (rejoicing in Italian), or as a corruption of the Latin *sponsalia* (the Roman engagement party).[21]

The *nissuin* ceremony was held at the groom's or his father's home in the Talmudic period and the *huppah* denoted the nuptial tent or room where the vows were consummated. In medieval Germany the wedding ceremony was shifted to the synagogue and the *huppah* now consisted of spreading or covering the bridal couple with a cloth (*sudar*) or a prayer shawl (*tallit*).[22] It is worth noting that in Christian usage, during the nuptial Mass in the church, a cloth (*pallium, valamen, velum*) was also spread over the bridal couple. This Christian custom is already found in Germany in the early Middle Ages and it is likely that Jews adopted this practice.[23]

The nuptial custom of breaking a glass at the conclusion of the wedding ceremony can also be traced to medieval Germany and is found in the Rhineland as early as the twelfth century.[24] Tradition later tried to justify the custom by claiming that it served as a reminder of the destruction of Jerusalem (*zekher lahurban*).[25] The glass used for the wedding benedictions was thrown at the northern wall of the synagogue during the Middle Ages.[26] Similar customs of smashing a glass at weddings were at home in medieval Christian Germany as popular belief held that the thrown glass would smash the power of the demons residing in the northern region.[27]

In the wake of the brutal massacres visited on Jews during the Crusades (from 1096 on) and later during the Black Plague (1348–1349), memorializations of the dead became an important aspect of medieval German Jewish life, and several ceremonies—*yizkor,* the *mourner's kaddish,* and *Jahrzeit*—evolved to assume a significant role in Ashkenazi Judaism. These rites, too, clearly reveal their indebtedness to contemporary Christian practices.

Two distinct commemorations developed in medieval Germany; Solomon Freehof calls them "The Communal Martyr Liturgy" and "The Communal Family Liturgy." The Communal Martyr Liturgy consisted of reading the *Memor*-lists or martyrology to commemorate the *kedoshim* ("saints") who had chosen martyrdom for the sanctification of God (*kiddush ha-Shem*). The Sabbath before the late spring *Shavuot* (Penteost) and the Sabbath nearest the midsummer *Tish'ah b'Av* were chosen in medieval Germany for the memorialization of martyrs. Alongside this rite, there developed in medieval Germany what is now called *yizkor* or *hazkarat neshamot* (prayer for the souls of the dead)—the "Communal Family Liturgy"—which memorialized the dead on *Yom Kippur* (the Day of Atonement). Prayer and charity, it was held, can speed the redemption of the dead and enable the dead souls to obtain rest in paradise.[28] These two rites find earlier Christian parallels in the "Feast of All Saints" (or "All Saints' Day") and "All Souls' Day." On "All Saints' Day" the commemoration consisted of reciting lists of saints (martyrology), many of whom had been martyred for the sanctification of Christ. "All Souls' Day" was the solemn commemoration of all the departed faithful. Charity and prayer, it was believed, would help the deceased souls, perhaps lingering in purgatory, attain the final purification necessary for admission to the beatific vision.[29] It should be observed that the very name *Memorbuch* (memorial book) comes from the Latin *memoria* (memory) and that the prayer which follows the Christian recitation of the departed begins with *memento* (remember), just as the Hebrew prayer begins with *yizkor* (remember).[30]

The *kaddish* prayer is now popularly thought of as a prayer for the dead. In reality it is a doxology, whose content reveals no link with death or with praying for the dead. The idea that the recitation of the *kaddish* prayer by the living has the power to atone for the sins of the deceased and to redeem the dead from *gehinnom* (Gehenna) is first indicated in twelfth and thirteenth century Rhenish sources.[31] Again, this prayer has its roots in the Requiem Mass or Mass for the dead celebrated in the Church so that through prayer and sacrifice the living can aid the souls in purgatory and help them attain eternal glory.[32]

The *Jahrzeit* (i.e., anniversary of a death) observance—the recitation of the *kaddish,* usually by the orphan, on the anniversary of his parent's death—is an established custom by the fourteenth century in southern Germany and the German word *Jahrzeit* is encountered in a responsum of the fifteenth century German rabbi, Moses Minz.[33] Similarly, the custom of lighting a memorial candle on the anniversary of the departed is recorded in the fifteenth century,[34] but the word *Jahrzeitlicht* (or *ner-Jahrzeit,* anniversary candle or light) and its burning for twenty-four hours is found in Jewish sources no earlier than the seventeenth century.[35] The designation *Jahrzeit* was used in the Christian Church to indicate the annual time for honoring the dead at anniversary Masses.[36] It was also customary at that time to light votive candles in both the home and church in memory of the departed.[37]

There can be little doubt that Christianity exerted a profound influence on the development of the Ashkenazi life cycle customs and ceremonies in medieval Germany. This should not be surprising, as the Jewish involvement with Christian civilization produced a unique and novel Judaism—Ashkenazi Judaism—just as previous Judaisms unmistakably bear the hallmark of their involvement with Islamic and Hellenistic civilizations. It was not the intention of this study to present an exhaustive treatment of all medieval Ashkenazi customs—so lovingly recorded in medieval Ashkenazi *minhagim* books[38]—and their Christian counterparts. Rather, it is hoped that my remarks will encourage scholars of comparative religion, folklore, liturgy, rabbinics and patristics to probe more deeply into a fascinating area of research, which has for understandable reasons been sadly neglected to date.

NOTES

1. *Sefer Hasidim,* No. 1101, (ed. R. Margoliot, Jerusalem, 1964), 557.

2. Cf. the excellent study of I.G. Marcus, *Piety and Society. The Jewish Pietists of Medieval Germany* (Leiden, 1981). Cf. the review by J. Dan in *Tarbiz* 51 (1982), 319–325 (in Hebrew).

3. E. Rivkin, *The Shaping of Jewish History. A Radical New Interpretation* (New York, 1971), 119ff., and G. Kisch, *The Jews of Medieval Germany. A Study of their Legal and Social Status* (New York, 1970[2]).

4. Cf. E. Rivkin, "The Writing of Jewish History," *The Reconstruction* 25 (June 15 and 26), 13–18, 24–27.

5. M. Güdemann, *Geschichte des Erziehungswesens und der Cultur der abendländischen Juden,* III (Wien, 1888, Amsterdam, 1966[2]), and L. Löw, *Die Lebensalter in der jüdischen Literatur* (Szegedin, 1875).

6. E. Rivkin, "The Utilization of Non-Jewish Sources for the Reconstruction of Jewish History," *The Jewish Quarterly Review,* 48 (1957), 183.

7. On Lilith, cf. J. Dan, "Samuel, Lilith and the Concept of Evil in Early

Kabbalah," *AJS Review,* 5 (1980), 17–40; J. Morgenstern, *Rites of Birth, Marriage, Death and Kindred Occasions among the Semites* (Cincinnati, 1960), 19ff.; T. Gaster, *The Holy and the Profane* (New York, 1955), 18ff.

8. O. Schnitzler, "Jüdischc Beschneidungsamulette aus Süddeutschland, dem Elsass, der Schweiz und aus Hessen," *Schweizerisches Archiv für Volkskunde,* 74 (1978), 41–45; M.L. Bamberger, "Aus meiner Minhagimsammelmappe," *Jahrbuch für jüdische Volkskunde,* 1 (1923), 323–24.

9. Güdemann, *op. cit.,* 103ff., n. 2 for other words used for this night, such as *leil shimurim, Waizen-Nacht, shalom zakhar.* Cf. also J.D. Eisenstein, "Wachnacht," *The Jewish Encyclopedia,* XII (New York, 1906), 454–55; H. Pollack, *Jewish Folkways in Germanic Lands (1648–1806)* (Cambridge, Mass., 1971), 19, 214, nn. 34–35 and Gaster, *op. cit.,* 60ff.

10. *Sefer Maharil, Hilkhot Berit-Milah* (Benei Berak, 1958/59), 100. Pollack, *op. cit.,* 18–19, 213 for variations of this custom. Cf. Gaster, *op. cit.,* 61ff. The ceremony was called Judsch Kerz, because circumcision was the act of making the boy Jewish. Cf. also Bamberger, *op. cit.,* 327. W.M. Christiani, *Bet ha-Kenesset, oder Kurtze Beschreibung einer wohleingerichteten Synagog* (Regensburg, 1723), 24–25 speaks of a Milah-Kerze made of twelve colored intertwined strands of wax in honor of the twelve tribes. I have been unable to find Gaster's source for the identification of the big candle with Jacob. More likely the *ner-tamid* referred to by Jacob Möllin is the *Shekhinah* (= God). *Ner-tamid* also refers to the memorial candle (*neshamah Licht*) lit in the synagogue on *Yom Kippur.* Cf. A. Margaritha, *Der gantze jüdische Glaube* (Leipzig, 1705), 72. Only from the seventeenth century on does a *ner-tamid* (eternal light) burn before the Torah Ark; cf. J. Gutmann, "How Traditional Are Our Traditions?" in J. Gutmann, ed., *Beauty in Holiness: Studies in Jewish Customs and Ceremonial Art* (New York, 1970), 417. This custom was influenced by Christianity where eternal lights burned before or in the Tabernacle housing the sacrament. The eternal light symbolized the corporeal presence of Christ, the light of the world; cf. S. and A. Ress, "Ewiges Licht (christlich)," *Reallexikon zur deutschen Kunstgeschichte,* VI (1973), 600–17. Cf. also E. Roth, "Das Licht im jüdischen Brauchtum, *Udim,* 3 (1972), 82ff. and 103ff.

11. Pollack, *op. cit.,* 18–19 and Gaster, *op. cit.,* 62.

12. Moses Minz, *Responsa,* Nos. 19, 37, 64. Cf. Güdemann, *op. cit.,* 104. Moses Minz, who lived in fifteenth century Germany, gave the explanation he had heard from his father. Cf. H. Schauss, *The Lifetime of a Jew Throughout the Ages of Jewish History* (Cincinnati, 1950), 44ff.; Gaster, *op. cit.,* 36ff.; Pollack, *op. cit.,* 27 and 217ff.; E. Roth "On the Hol-Kreisch," *Yeda'Am,* 7 (1960), 66–69 (in Hebrew); Bamberger, *op cit.,* 328–29. For the actual prayers recited during the ceremony, cf. *Seder Hol-Kreisch* in L. Wolff, *Universal-Agende für jüdische Kultusbeamte* (Berlin, 1891), 39–40.

13. A. Landau, "Hollekreisch," *Zeitschrift des Vereins für Völkerkunde,* 9 (1899), 72–77; A. Wuttke, *Der deutsche Aberglaube der Gegenwart* (Berlin, 1900), 24ff.

14. Cf. the sources cited in S.B. Freehof, "Ceremonial Creativity among the Ashkenazim," Gutmann, *Beauty in Holiness,* 493ff.

15. D.A. Maloney, "Confirmation," and P.T. Camelot, "Confirmation in Grace," *New Catholic Encyclopedia,* IV (New York, 1967), 145ff.

16. H.J. Zimmels, *Ashkenazim and Sephardim* (London, 1958), 176ff.

17. Cf. K. Ritzer, *Formen, Riten und religiöses Brauchtum der Eheschliessung in den christlichen Kirchen des ersten Jahrtausends* (Münster, 1962), 132, 253ff. and J.W. Falk, *Jewish Matrimonial Law in the Middle Ages* (London, 1966), 77, 84; Gaster, *op. cit.,* 84.

18. Schauss, *op. cit.,* 182ff.; Güdemann, *op. cit.,* 119; Pollack, *op. cit.,* 29–30, 218–19, nn. 82ff.; J. Gutmann, "Wedding Customs and Ceremonies in Art," in Gutmann, *Beauty in Holiness,* 316; A. Fürst, *Sitten und Gebräuche einer Judengasse* (Szekesfehervas, 1908), 53ff.

19. *Sefer Maharil, Hilkhot Tish'ah b'Av,* 65.

20. Güdemann, *op. cit.,* 119ff.; Schauss, *op. cit.,* 166, 175ff.; Pollack, *op. cit.,* 32ff., 220, nn. 98–99.

21. Different *Spinnholz* ceremonies apparently existed in Germany. In Frankfurt [Joseph Yuspa Hahn (? –1637), *Yosif Ometz* (Jerusalem, 1964/65), No. 657, p. 146] two *Spinnholz* ceremonies were celebrated on two preceding Sabbaths, known as the "Little" and the "Great *Spinnholz.*"

22. Cf. S.B. Freehof, "The Chuppah," in D.J. Silver, ed., *In the Time of Harvest* (New York, 1963), 186–93 and *idem, Modern Reform Responsa* (Cincinnati, 1971), 294–99; Schauss, *op. cit.,* 155ff. and 171ff.

23. Ritzer, *op. cit.,* 158ff., 176, 194, 231f.; Güdemann, *op. cit.,* 121, n. 4; Gaster, *op. cit.,* 113. The current use of a portable canopy (*huppah*), an awning of cloth upheld by four poles, was also adopted from the Church. Cf. J. Sauer, *Symbolik des Kirchengebäudes und seiner Auffassung des Mittelalters* (Freiburg, 1924), 210.

24. J.Z. Lauterbach, "The Ceremony of Breaking a Glass at Weddings," in Gutmann, *Beauty in Holiness,* 340–69; Freehof, "Ceremonial Creativity," 491–93. Early sources indicate that the second cup over which the *birkhot nissuin* (the nuptial benedictions) had been recited was shattered; later the cup over which the betrothal benediction (*birkat erusin*) had been read was broken; cf. Lauterbach, *op. cit.,* 358ff. The shouting of *mazzal tov* at the ceremony appears to be first recorded by the fifteenth century German rabbi, Moses Minz, *Responsa,* No. 109, but at that time it was uttered after the *birkat erusin* and not at the conclusion of the wedding ceremonies.

25. Lauterbach, *op. cit.,* 360 [*Kolbo, Hilkhot Tish'ah b'Av* (Venice, 1547), 67]. Cf. also Moses Minz, *Responsa* No. 109.

26. Gutmann, "Wedding Customs," 318.

27. Wuttke, *op. cit.,* 210, 369; Lauterbach, *op. cit.,* 364f.; Gaster, *op. cit.,* 119–121.

28. S.B. Freehof, "Hazkarath Neshamoth," *Hebrew Union College Annual,* 36 (1965), 179–89.

29. A. Cornides, "All Souls' Day," and C. Smith, "All Saints, Feast of," *New Catholic Encyclopedia,* I, 318ff.

30. Cf. Gaster, *op. cit.,* 185ff.; Schauss, *op. cit.,* 299; Pollack, *op. cit.,* 43, 47.

31. Freehof, "Ceremonial Creativity," 488–91; Schauss, *op. cit.,* 294ff. Cf. the interesting comment by the twelfth century Spanish Jewish scholar, Abraham bar Hiyya: "Anyone who believes that after his death he can be benefited by the actions of his sons and their prayers for him is harboring false ideas (i.e., self-delusion)": Freehof; *ibid.,* 490–91.

32. A. Cornides, "Requiem Mass, Liturgy of," *New Catholic Encyclopedia,* XII, 384ff.

33. Moses Minz, *Responsa* No. 80. Cf. Freehof, "Ceremonial Creativity," 490.

34. *Leket Yosher,* I (Berlin, 1903), 32, 49. Roth, *op. cit.,* 109f.

35. Ya'ir Hayyim Bacharach (1639–1702) writes: "One should not mock a custom, even though there is no reason [for its existence], as is the case with the *Jahrzeit* candle." Güdemann, *op. cit.,* 128 and S. Freehof, *Reform Jewish Practice and Its Rabbinic Background,* I (Cincinnati, 1944), 156; Pollack, *op. cit.,* 230, n. 170.

36. Cornides, *op. cit.,* 384. Cf. Güdemann, *op. cit.,* 132, n. 1: " 'Jahrzeitbuch' (anniversarium) hiess das Verzeichnis der an bestimmten Tagen zu lesenden Seelenmessen."

37. P. Sartori, "Feuer und Licht im Totengebrauche," *Zeitschrift des Vereins für Völkerkunde,* 17 (1907), 382; Schauss, *op. cit.,* 297.

38. Solomon Freehof pointed out: "There are no such biographical ceremonial-diaries in Sephardic Jewish literature," in "Ceremonial Creativity," 499. Cf. S. Steiman, *Custom and Survival* (New York, 1963), 3ff.

8.
The Influence of Jewish Liturgical Spirituality on Christian Traditions: Some Observations

Eugene J. Fisher

In encouraging representatives of episcopal conferences from around the world to intensify dialogue and collaboration with the Jewish community as "people of God," Pope John Paul II centered especially on the liturgy:

> Such relationships can and ought to help enrich the knowledge of our own roots and to shed more light on certain aspects of this identity of which we speak. Our common spiritual heritage with Jews is considerable. Help in better understanding certain aspects of the Church's life can be gained by taking an inventory of that heritage, and also by taking into account the faith and religious life of the Jewish people as professed and lived now as well. This is the case with the liturgy. Its roots have still to be more deeply traced, and above all need to be better known and appreciated by the faithful . . . for they have been inspired ever since the beginning of the Church by certain aspects of the synagogue's community organization (Rome, March 6, 1982).

Christian spirituality, communal as well as individual, is said here not only to find its source in biblical Judaism, but to have been constantly enriched over the centuries by Jewish spirituality and Jewish liturgical developments. That this should be so, despite the traditional hesitancy of both religious communities to acknowledge the mutual sharing of ways of approaching God and of responding to God's call to loving encounter, is in retrospect quite understandable.

Christians worship, not just any God, but quite specifically the One God, the God of Israel, the God of Abraham and Sarah, Isaac and Rebecca, Jacob and Rachel. We are taught to address God in prayer, not by just any title, but by quite specifically Jewish titles, particularly God as "Father," a designation reflecting the covenant relationship itself.

Obviously, an article of this length cannot hope to do justice to the complexity of its topic, especially when so many critical areas, as the Pope hints, are only now beginning to receive the scholarly and detailed attention they deserve. The appended bibliography, it is hoped, will be of some help to the reader interested in pursuing the thoughts offered in this way. In the meantime, only the briefest survey of some selected points of contact between the two traditions can be attempted here.

1. JESUS AND JEWISH PRAYER

Jesus was a Jew who prayed as a Jew. So it should come as no surprise that he taught his followers to pray as Jews: "This is how you are to pray: Our Father . . ." (Mt 6:9–13; cf. Lk 4:2–4). It has been shown[1] that each of the elements of this primary Christian prayer finds a close parallel in biblical and especially rabbinic literature. Further, while the analogy of God's Fatherhood of Israel is found throughout the Hebrew Scriptures as constitutive of Jewish peoplehood (e.g., Ex 4:22f; Dt 30:9; 32:5; Hos 2:1; 11:1; Jer 3:19; 31:9, 20; Is 1:4; 63:16; 64:7; Mal 1:6), it is not until the later period that it begins to be used as a title in prayer (Sir 23:1, 4; 51:10). And it is not until rabbinic Judaism, toward the end of the first century, that the designation of God as "your" ("my") "Father in heaven" is attested.[2]

This latter designation (never without the qualifying pronoun) occurs some twenty times in Matthew, once in Mark (11:25), but not at all in Luke (though see Lk 11:13). While the time gap in the transmission of these liturgical traditions (Targumic and New Testament) renders impossible any attempt to conclude that Jesus' usage is dependent upon the rabbinic (or, for that matter, vice versa), it does show that his style of prayer most likely reflects not only general Jewish forms of prayer, but particular rabbinic-Pharisaic forms. Indeed, the very context of the Our Father in Matthew (6:1–7, 16–18) exemplifies Jesus' quite Pharisaic concern for the purity of intention in synagogue prayer and fasting.

Recently, Joachim Jeremias[3] has made much of Jesus' use of the term

"Abba" ("O Father") to address God (Mk 14:36) during the agony in the garden. Jeremias attempts to develop this "Abba experience" into a major dividing point between Jesus' spirituality and that of his fellow Jews.[4] This, however, seems to be a rather elaborate theology to derive from a single Gospel reference. The term "Abba" is itself simply an emphatic Aramaic equivalent of *'ab* ("Father"), employed as a vocative.[5] Ancient Aramaic and even contemporary Hebrew sources indicate that it was used as a familiar address by children. The use of it as a prayer formula among early Christians is attested twice in the Epistles (Rom 8:15; Gal 4:6), where it reflects the early Church's post-resurrection understanding of Jesus. It was not a prayer-tradition taught by Jesus himself[6] to his disciples.

The passages from Romans and Galatians, however, while not justifying all that Jeremias might wish to build upon them, do point to a central difference between Jewish and Christian spirituality. Christian liturgical tradition is imbued from its earliest days not only with the faith of Jesus, but also with faith *in* Jesus as the risen Lord, a teaching and a mystery which Judaism cannot accept. On the other hand, it needs to be recalled precisely at this deepest point of divergence, as Clemens Thoma reminds us, that even here we pray "as Jesus taught us":

> A further convergence can be detected in the fact that the New Testament and liturgical doxologies (Rom 11:33–36 and the final doxology of the Roman Canon) and all the "classic" liturgical prayers are not directed to Jesus but to the "Father."[7]

2. THE SYNAGOGUE AND THE CHURCH AT WORSHIP

It is not my point here to attempt to go through in detail all of the parallels indicating the origins of Christian liturgy in Jewish practice. Sofia Cavalletti's summary of the Jewish roots of Christian liturgy remains perhaps the best brief introduction in English to date[8] of this question. Some basic points, however, might be noted to set the detailed discussion in a wider context.

Perhaps the first thing that strikes one approaching it is a remarkable passage from the Book of Acts. Immediately following the first Christian Pentecost and Peter's discourse, Acts describes the life of the early Church:

> They devoted themselves to the apostles' instruction and the communal life, to the breaking of bread and the prayers. . . . They went to the

> temple area together every day, while in their homes they broke bread. With exultant and sincere hearts they took their meals in common, praising God and winning the approval of all the people (Acts 2:42, 46–47).

It is clear here that not only did the first Christians continue to view themselves as Jews, but that they were accepted as such by other Jews and that their form of worship remained Jewish. It was only very gradually that Christians began to adapt Jewish customs and rituals to their own unique vision of "being with" the Father. It must be remembered that just as the early Church was transforming the common biblical heritage, so too was Judaism developing, particularly through the rabbis, to meet the crises of Jewish history. Hence, it is not so much that Christianity is a derivative of rabbinic Judaism but that the two developed, side by side, in uneasy togetherness, out of that one biblical stock, each evolving its own unique responses to what were, often enough, common problems of history.

This is not to say that the Church's liturgy did not evolve primarily out of the synagogue or that its primary point of reference was not Pharisaic/Rabbinic Judaism. The synagogue and its attendant liturgical innovations pre-date the New Testament period by some time, as does the Pharisaic movement.[9] Perhaps it is because of the very closeness of the Jesus and Pharisaic movements that such bitterness as is reflected in the Gospel of Matthew ultimately developed between them.

The term for "Church," *ecclesia,* is like "synagogue," an equivalent for the Hebrew *kahal,* "assembly." Thus the intimate relationship of the two religious movements at some point is attested in their basic ways of gathering together for prayer and communal life. It was the synagogue and its structures that provided Christians no less than Jews with theoretical and organizational models for developing ways of worshiping the Father when the Temple (which Jesus loved and which the early Christians attended) was finally destroyed in the year 70 of the common era.

It was not that the synagogue represented a rival institution to the Temple. There were synagogues in Jerusalem (Acts 6:9; 24:12), even in the Temple area itself.[10] And rabbinic literature such as the *Mishnah* (e.g., 6:1) looks back on the Temple with nostalgia and with a precise recollection of its rites. Rather, beginning with the Babylonian exile and the exilic prophets (e.g., Dn 3:38–41 in the Septuagint), spiritual practices in regard to interior dispositions, repentance, prayer and charity, as well as a cycle of scriptural readings and study conforming to the Temple cycle, were being observed by many Jews. Christianity quite naturally picked up these basically Pharisaic approaches to prayer and worship.

Liturgical prayer by the gathered community in the Presence of God, then, was not limited exclusively to the Temple even in ancient Judaism, much less in Jesus' time. The saying of Jesus, which appears to define the liturgical community, that "where two or three are gathered in my name . . ." (Mt 18:20) is paralleled in a series of Talmudic dicta.

> Rabin b. R. Adda says in the name of Rabbi Isaac: How do you know that the Holy One, blessed be He, is to be found in the Synagogue? For it is said: God stands in the congregation of God (Ps 82:1). And how do you know that if ten people pray together the Divine Presence is with them? For it is said: God stands in the congregation of God (i.e., the *minyan,* see Sanh. 2b). And how do you know that if two are sitting and studying Torah together the Divine Presence is with them? For it is said: Then they that feared the Lord spoke with one another, and the Lord hearkened and heard (Mal 3:16). And how do you know that even if one man sits and studies the Torah the Divine Presence is with him? For it is said: In every place where I cause my Name to be mentioned I will come unto thee and bless thee (Ex 20:21).[11]

Similar sayings can be found in the Talmud which equate good deeds and prayer with the Temple sacrifice. Just as the Epistle to the Hebrews effectively replaces the Temple ritual with what came to be interpreted as a sacramental joining of the community with the salvific death and resurrection of Christ, so too did the synagogue provide more than adequately for a "Temple-less" cult and direct access to the divine Presence, stressing the essentiality of the proper spirit and intention over the externals alone.

3. THE ORDER OF PRAYER

It is well known today that the Christian order of the Eucharist takes its form and structure from combining key elements of the traditional synagogue service (the Liturgy of the Word) with elements of the Jewish Passover meal.[12] Likewise, it is relatively easy to discern the Jewish background of the Christian liturgical cycle. Easter and Pentecost, of course, are basically adaptations (with dates modified according to the solar calendar following the Gregorian reform) of the Jewish spring festivals of Passover and Pentecost, as the liturgy itself acknowledges. In both cases essential themes, as well as specific Scripture readings and customs, have simply been taken over by the Church and shifted to a Christological setting, often without disturbing the underlying spiritual motifs involved.

The great Jewish autumn cycle of New Year and Yom Kippur (Day of Atonement) is also remarkably parallel in theme and content to the beginning of the Christian year with Advent and Christmas. In the early Church, Advent, a period of preparation for the spiritual renewal of the liturgical New Year, lasted six weeks, corresponding to the six "Sabbaths of Preparation" of the Jewish calendar in the same period.[13] St. Jerome himself associated Christmas with the Jewish New Year because both celebrated renewal. Basic themes, such as the penitential emphasis and the use of prophetic readings, particularly from Isaiah (e.g., Is 40:1–26 and 60:1–22), which offer the vision of messianic hope, are also common to the two cycles. As Cavalletti comments, "This complex of elements common to the celebration of Christmas and to the Jewish New Year cannot be explained as the result of chance,"[14] an impression solidified by the similarities between two other festivals of the same cycle, Epiphany and Sukkoth. Both Epiphany, especially as celebrated in Eastern Christianity (which often preserves a closer bond with Jewish liturgy than does that of the West), and Tabernacles (Sukkoth) include celebrations of water and light. Interestingly, the introduction of the element of a display of lights on Sukkoth (*Mishna,* Sukkah 5, 3), an element which features prominently in Eastern Christian Epiphany, was called by the rabbis "the great innovation of the Pharisees."

Beyond the annual cycle, specific sacraments, such as baptism, with its obvious adaptation of the purifying ritual of the *mikvah,* and the marriage liturgy also derive essential themes and ritual elements from Jewish tradition. The Christian concept of marriage as symbolically reflective of both the order of creation and the covenant relationship between God and His people is certainly derived from Jewish antecedents. Again, it is of interest that the celebration of the sacrament in the Eastern Church, with its deep rootage in the Hebrew Scriptures, is closely allied with the Jewish celebration in many particulars, as Adrien Nocent has recently shown.[15] Even the eschatological imagery of marriage as found in Jesus' teaching (e.g., Mt 22:1–14), can be seen in such Jewish customs as the royal attire of the groom and bride, the procession, and the shared meal ending in hymns of joy, a joy made all the more poignant by the breaking of the wine cup as a reminder that Israel remains unredeemed in the present, its Temple destroyed.[16]

Finally, a word needs to be said concerning the convergence and divergence of what are doubtlessly the central feasts of the two traditions: the Sabbath and Sunday. The Eastern Churches in the early centuries, with the exception of Alexandria, kept the Sabbath as a day of liturgical assembly, banning fasting on it as a profanation just as did rabbinic tradition.[17] It may be that Sunday worship in Christianity originally developed as a sequel and conclusion to the Sabbath synagogue service, with the faithful gathering for the breaking of bread after the close of the Sabbath at sunset to avoid traveling on the Sabbath itself. If so, this would help to explain both the practice of breaking bread at night (Acts 20) and the sense of continuity of the two weekly feasts.

Both Sabbath and Sunday contain a dynamic tension between the celebration of creation[18] and an eschatological foretaste of the Kingdom of God. Though it was not until the fourth century, when Constantine ordered Sunday to be observed as a day of rest, that Sunday took on this biblical aspect for Western Christians, the practice has raised the issue of Sunday as a day of rest ever since. Also from the fourth century, according to Nocent, "there begins a theology of Sunday as the first day, that of creation, and at the same time of the eighth day, that of the Parousia."[19] Again, one notes a Christian equivalent of the Jewish theology of the Sabbath.

Sabbath and Sunday, like Judaism and Christianity themselves, are profoundly related spiritual realities. But they are not the same reality. Each has its distinctive meaning which can be illumined by dialogue with, but never subsumed into, the other. This article has provided only the sketchiest outline of the dialogue that needs to take place between our two traditions on liturgical matters. It is a dialogue, I would argue, that both "sides" of the interreligious equation should look forward to with openness and anticipation. For in it the spirituality of both traditions can come to be better understood and enriched.

NOTES

1. E. Fisher, *Faith Without Prejudice,* 51 (cf. I. Abrahams, *Studies in Pharisaism,* 98–99. For complete references for these and other works cited, see the Bibliography, below).

2. M. McNamara, *Targum and Testament,* 115. McNamara lists and analyzes the major Targumic occurrences.

3. J. Jeremias, *The Parables of Jesus* (London: SCM, 1963), *New Testament Theology* (London: SCM, 1971) and *The Prayers of Jesus* (London: SCM, 1974).

4. See J. Pawlikowski, *Christ in the Light of the Christian-Jewish Dialogue,* 103.

5. J.L. McKenzie, *Dictionary of the Bible* (Milwaukee: Bruce, 1965) 1.

6. On this question, see also J. Oesterreicher, "Abba, Father: On the Humanity of Jesus," in M. Brocke and J. Petuchowski, eds., *The Lord's Prayer and Jewish Liturgy,* 119–136.

7. C. Thoma, *A Christian Theology of Judaism,* 104.

8. See Bibliography.

9. Louis Finkelstein in *New Light from the Prophets* (N.Y.: Basic Books, 1969) sees the origins of the synagogue in the exigencies of maintaining the cult in the absence of the Temple during the Babylonian exile, and the origins of the Pharisaic/Rabbinic movement in the prophets of the exilic period.

10. R. Le Déaut, *et al., The Spirituality of Judaism,* 30.

11. T.B. *Berakoth* 6a (Soncino translation).

12. Cf. E. Fisher, *Faith Without Prejudice,* 104–105; S. Cavalletti, 14–22.

13. As it still does in the Ambrosian rite.

14. Cavalletti, 25.

15. A. Nocent, "The Contribution of Judaism to the Christian Liturgy of Marriage" (*SIDIC* 14:1, 1981) 11–19.

16. Cf. A. Finkel, "The Jewish Liturgy of Marriage" (*SIDIC* 14:1, 1981) 4–10. But cf. also J. Gutmann, this volume, p. 133.

17. The *Constitutiones Apostolicae* (VII: 23, 34), in the words of Cavalletti, "consider the Sabbath as a festal day like Sunday, the first commemorating creation and the second the resurrection" (*ibid.,* 23).

18. *Didascalia apostolorum* VI, 18, 11–15; Eusebius, *Sermones* 16 (p. 208, no. 135); Justin, *Apologia* 1, 67, 7. Cf. L. Klenicki, this volume, p. 13.

19. A. Nocent, "*The Christian Sunday*" (SIDIC, Vol. X: 1, 1977) 12.

AN INTRODUCTORY BIBLIOGRAPHY

Anniyil, N.T., "An Ancient Biblical Spirituality: The Liturgy of Malankara Catholics of India," *The Bible Today* (Vol. 20:4, 1982) 237–242.

Bacehiochi, Samuele, *From Sabbath to Sunday* (Rome: Pontifical Gregorian University, 1977).

Baumstark, Anton, *Comparative Liturgy* (London, 1958).

Bouyer, L., "Jewish and Christian Liturgies," in L. Sheppard, ed., *True Worship* (Baltimore: Helicon Press, 1963) 29–44.

Brocke, M., and Petuchowski, J., *The Lord's Prayer and Jewish Liturgy* (New York: Seabury, 1978).

Cavalletti, Sofia, "Christian Liturgy: Its Roots in Judaism," *SIDIC* (Rome: Vol. 6:1, 1973) 10–28.

Finkel, Asher, "The Passover Story and the Last Supper," in M. Zeig and M. Siegel, eds., *Root and Branch* (Roth Publ., 1973) 19–46.

Fisher, Eugene, "Continuity and Discontinuity in the Lectionary Readings," *Liturgy* (May, 1978) 30–37.

———, "The Liturgy of Lent and Christian-Jewish Relations," *Ecumenical Trends* (March, 1981) 36–40.

———, "From Theory to Praxis: Education Through Liturgy," *SIDIC* (Rome: Vol. 15:2, 1982) 11–16.

———, and Daniel Polish, eds., *Liturgical Foundations for Social Policy in the Catholic and Jewish Traditions* (South Bend: University of Notre Dame Press, 1983).

Flusser, David, "Notes on Easter and the Passover Haggadah," *Immanuel* (Jerusalem: No. 7, 1977) 52–61.

———, "Tensions Between Sabbath and Sunday," *SIDIC* (Rome: Vol. 10:1, 1977) 13–16.

Gavin, Frank, *The Jewish Antecedents of the Christian Sacraments* (London: SPCK, 1982).

Hoffmann, Lawrence, "A Symbol of Salvation in the Passover Haggadah," *Worship* (Vol. 53:6) 519–537.

Klenicki, Leon, "Creation and Freedom in the Celebration of the Sabbath," *The Liturgical Conference,* 1977.

———, ed., *The Passover Celebration* (Chicago: Liturgy Training Publications; New York: Anti-Defamation League of B'nai B'rith, 1980).

Le Déaut, Roger, *The Message of the N.T. and the Aramaic Bible* (Targum) (Rome: Biblical Inst. Press, 1982). Original French title: *Prière Juive et Nouveau Testament* (1965).

———, Jaubert, A., and Hruby, K., *The Spirituality of Judaism* (St. Meinrad, Ind.: Abbey Press, 1977) esp. pp. 25–40.

Nocent, A., "The Contribution of Judaism to the Christian Liturgy of Marriage," *SIDIC* (Rome: Vol. 14:1, 1981) 11–19.

Oesterley, W.O., *The Jewish Background of the Christian Liturgy* (Oxford: Clarendon Press, 1925).

Pawlikowski, J., *Christ in the Light of the Christian-Jewish Dialogue,* A Stimulus Book (New York: Paulist Press, 1982).

Rijk, C.A., "The Importance of Jewish-Christian Relations for Christian Liturgy," *SIDIC* (Rome: Vol. 6:1, 1973) 29–34.

Talley, Thos. J., "From Berakah to Eucharistia," *Worship* (Vol. 50:2, 1976) 115–137.

Tanenbaum, M.H., "Holy Year and Jewish Jubilee Year," *SIDIC* (Rome: Vol. 7:3, 1974) 4–12.

Thoma, C., *A Christian Theology of Judaism,* A Stimulus Book (New York: Paulist Press, 1980).

Werner, Eric, *The Sacred Bridge: Liturgical Parallels in the Synagogue and the Early Church* (New York: Schocken, 1970).

Notes on the Contributors

DR. EUGENE J. FISHER is director of the Secretariat for Catholic-Jewish Relations of the National Conference of Catholic Bishops. He is author of *Faith Without Prejudice* (Paulist Press, 1977) and co-editor, with Rabbi Daniel F. Polish of the volume, *Formation of Social Policy in the Catholic and Jewish Traditions* (University of Notre Dame Press, 1980), as well as the author of over fifty articles for religious and educational journals. Recently, Dr. Fisher was named Consultor to the Vatican Commission for Religious Relations with the Jews. He chairs both the Israel Study Group and the Jewish/Christian/Muslim Trialogue Group sponsored by the Kennedy Institute of Ethics of Georgetown University, and is past president of the Chesapeake Bay region of the Society of Biblical Literature.

DR. JOSEPH GUTMANN is Professor of Art History, Wayne State University and Adjunct Curator, Detroit Institute of Arts. He is the author of sixteen books, among them *Beauty in Holiness, No Graven Images, The Image and the Word, Temple of Solomon,* and *Hebrew Manuscript Painting.* Dr. Gutmann was ordained at Hebrew Union College-Jewish Institute of Religion, Cincinnati and serves as rabbi to Congregation Solel, Brighton, Michigan.

GABE HUCK is director of Liturgy Training Publications (Chicago). He has worked in parish and diocesan positions involving liturgy and religious education and is the author of *A Book of Family Prayer, Liturgy with Style and Grace,* and several audio-visual presentations on worship.

MARGARET MARY KELLEHER is a doctoral candidate in Spirituality and Liturgy at the Catholic University of America. She is an Ursuline Sister who has taught in both academic and parish settings. She has published in *Liturgy,* the journal of the Liturgical Conference.

LEON KLENICKI, rabbi, is co-director of the Department of Interfaith Affairs of the Anti-Defamation League of B'nai B'rith. He is professor of Jewish Theology at Immaculate Conception Seminary, Mahwah, N.J. Rabbi Klenicki co-edited *Issues in the Jewish-Christian Dialogue* (A Stimulus Book, Paulist Press, 1979) and *Biblical Studies, Meeting Ground of Jews and Christians* (A Stimulus Book, Paulist Press, 1980). He also is associate editor of *Face to Face: An Interreligious Bulletin.*

RONALD LEWINSKI is a priest of the Roman Catholic Archdiocese of Chicago, associate pastor at St. Marcelline's Parish in Schaumburg, IL. He is director of the catechumenate in the Archdiocese and author of *Welcoming the New Catholic* and *A Guide for Sponsors.* Father Lewinski is the editor of *The Chicago Catechumenate.*

DR. MARK SEARLE is assistant professor of Liturgy at the University of Notre Dame. He is the author of *Christening: The Making of Christians* and *Liturgy Made Simple,* and editor of several collections of essays, including *Liturgy and Social Justice* and *Parish: Place for Worship.*

DR. NORMAN SOLOMON is rabbi of the Hampstead Synagogue, London, England.

Index of Authors and Subjects